COP ON THE BEAT

Officer Steven Mayfield in New York City

Upper Manhattan

COP ON THE BEAT

Officer Steven Mayfield in New York City

TEXT & PHOTOGRAPHS BY

Arlene Schulman

DUTTON BOOKS

NEW YORK

ACKNOWLEDGMENTS

An extraordinary thanks goes to Police Officer Steven Mayfield for his patience and good humor as I observed, examined, questioned, probed, and debated the details of his life on the beat and at home.

His colleagues at New York City's 34th Precinct deserve a note of thanks for their support, in particular Inspectors José Cordero and Terence Monahan. And thanks also to Lieutenants James Melendez and Stuart Levine for their unwavering encouragement.

Susan Van Metre, my editor, must be commended for her expertise and wry observations, and Karen Lotz for her enthusiasm for this project.

Library of Congress Cataloging-in-Publication Data
Schulman, Arlene.
Cop on the beat: officer Steven Mayfield in New York City/text and photographs by Arlene Schulman.
p. cm.
Summary: Presents the experiences of Steven Mayfield, a New York City
police officer whose beat includes the neighborhoods of Washington Heights and Inwood.
ISBN 0-525-47064-6 (Hardcover)
ISBN 0-525-46527-8 (Paperback)
1. Police—New York (State)—New York—Juvenile literature. 2. Mayfield, Steven.
[1. Mayfield, Steven. 2. Police. 3. New York (N.Y.)] I. Title
HV8148 .N5 S3856 2002
363.2'08741—dc21 2002002591

Published in the United States 2002 by Dutton Books,
a member of Penguin Putnam Inc.
345 Hudson Street, New York, New York 10014
www.penguinputnam.com

Designed by Irene Vandervoort
Printed in Hong Kong
First Edition
10 9 8 7 6 5 4 3 2 1

CONTENTS

COP ON THE BEAT

Officer Steven Mayfield in New York City

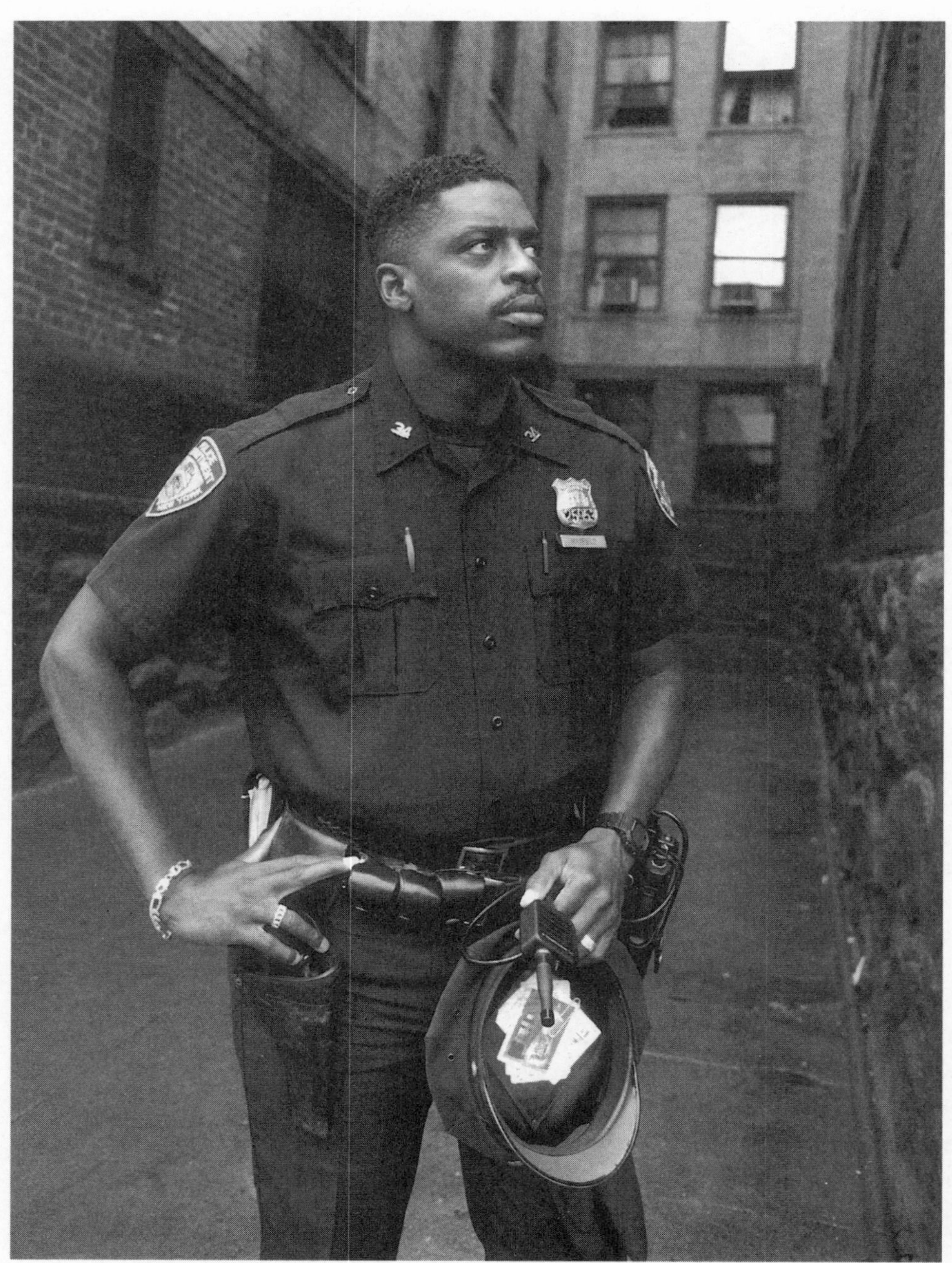

Officer Steven Mayfield in uniform

COP ON THE BEAT

His shoes are flawlessly shined, his shirt is precisely ironed and neatly tucked in, his shield gleams, and the creases in his dark blue pants stand so razor sharp they look dangerous. His pace varies from a cautious walk to a brisk run, through sheets of rain, mounds of snow, and the glare of a hot sun. His hat, its brim neatly dusted, usually conceals the top half of his eyes, making him a bit mysterious. His six-foot-three, 235-pound frame imposes but doesn't threaten. At night, he moves quietly among the dark shadows of trees and buildings, stepping out into the soft light of street lamps and disappearing back into the darkness. He moves so stealthily that local residents have dubbed him "the Shadow." But at the moment, something suspicious has caught the eye of New York City police officer Steven Mayfield, and he freezes.

Officer Mayfield is trained to react to emergencies, and now, his first day back at work after two days off, his instincts warn him to take action. He can handle this alone, but he cannot continue his patrol unless this small but offensive situation is quickly dealt with.

Mayfield picks a piece of lint off his dark blue uniform shirt. "Damn!" he groans. "Where did this come from?" He runs his hands over his shirt to be certain that the lint hasn't multiplied, and satisfied he is spotless again, he continues his walking patrol of his beat.

It's the third hour of his tour, which began at four this Tuesday afternoon. He will finish just after midnight. Officer Mayfield is a beat cop. Though he sometimes patrols in a car with a partner, he usually works alone, walking or

cycling the streets of the upper Manhattan neighborhoods of Washington Heights and Inwood. Beat officers like Mayfield carry a gun, a badge, a police radio, a flashlight, a nightstick, and handcuffs. They represent law and order in their small piece of New York City.

"People see how you present yourself," Mayfield says. "Image is everything. When I walk the streets, I'm very conscious of my appearance and how I look. Many people respect me because they've seen me in action. But for those who haven't, getting their respect has to do with how I carry myself, how I present myself, how I look. My appearance plays a big part," he says, pointing to his impeccably pressed pants, which he irons himself. "Size is not as important as most people think it is. What makes you and breaks you is how you carry yourself. If you're small but carry yourself in a proper manner, people are definitely not going to see you for your size," he adds.

The forty-year-old Mayfield tilts his head toward a patrol car across from the Dyckman Houses, a seven-building complex of affordable housing that makes up most of his beat. He watches critically as an officer from his own precinct, the 34th, leaves a ticket on a double-parked car. His fellow cop lifts up a windshield wiper, sticks the paper underneath, and closes his summons book with a snap. His next move makes Mayfield grimace. The cop hitches his pants up over his big belly, leaving a four-inch gap between cuffs and shoes. "I hate seeing men and women in that state," Mayfield groans, wondering if the man is wearing the wrong-size uniform or if he's gained weight. "He represents me just as I represent him. And I think I'm doing a fair job representing him. I would like him to do the same for me."

Mayfield walks farther up Dyckman Street toward Broadway. Cars are double-parked near *empty* parking spaces. Their drivers are in the nearby shops, buying a dress, shoes, or last-minute items. "Where's the common sense?" he exclaims, annoyed. "I don't understand why no one can pull into a space."

Officer Mayfield writes a summons for a double-parked car on Dyckman Street.

Someone has told the shoppers that the police are ticketing. People run out of stores, bumping into one another in the race to avoid a parking ticket. "Sir," Mayfield calls out to one driver, "why not pull into the space over there?

"Now I'm a parking attendant," he mutters to himself. One or two drivers aren't fast enough; he lifts windshield wipers to place summonses underneath and then continues up the street.

Mayfield is always on the lookout for crime, large and small—from parking violations to neighborhood robberies to fights with fists, knives, or guns. If he doesn't spot it himself, he may be called to the scene of a crime or emergency by a concerned neighbor or stranger, a passing cabdriver or truck driver, or by the police dispatcher, speaking over his portable police radio. Being a beat cop means being nearby when you're needed.

While he walks, Mayfield listens over car horns and other street sounds to the voice on his police radio. If the dispatcher calls out, "Beat eight"—the number of his beat—or an address in the vicinity, the job is his. Some days the dispatcher calls out job after job. On other days, the radio is surprisingly quiet. But it isn't the radio that is unpredictable . . . it's the emotions and actions of people that are. There is no anticipating when a man and woman might argue violently or a curious child might play with matches. At any moment, an apartment may be burglarized or someone around the corner might die. Mayfield has seen his share of emergencies. The saddest, he says, is sitting in an apartment alone with a dead body as he waits for the medical examiner to inspect the corpse and sign off on paperwork.

Officer Mayfield stops for dinner during his tour.

"No, I'm not afraid to see death," Mayfield says while he stops for dinner at a Dyckman Street pizzeria, neatly slicing into a dish of lasagna placed on the worn wooden table and carefully wiping the corners of his mouth with a white napkin. Some cops have seen less death than Mayfield, others more. While many say they are used to it, others admit that particular deaths stay with them.

Mayfield says, "I've had fresh corpses and I've had very old ones, bodies with maggots. You sit there and hope that the coroner and the funeral home get there soon. It's a somber atmosphere. I try and put the family at ease." He takes a gulp of Pepsi. "I remember one where a guy hung himself from a tree in the park. That had to be one of the worst ones I ever saw because his neck

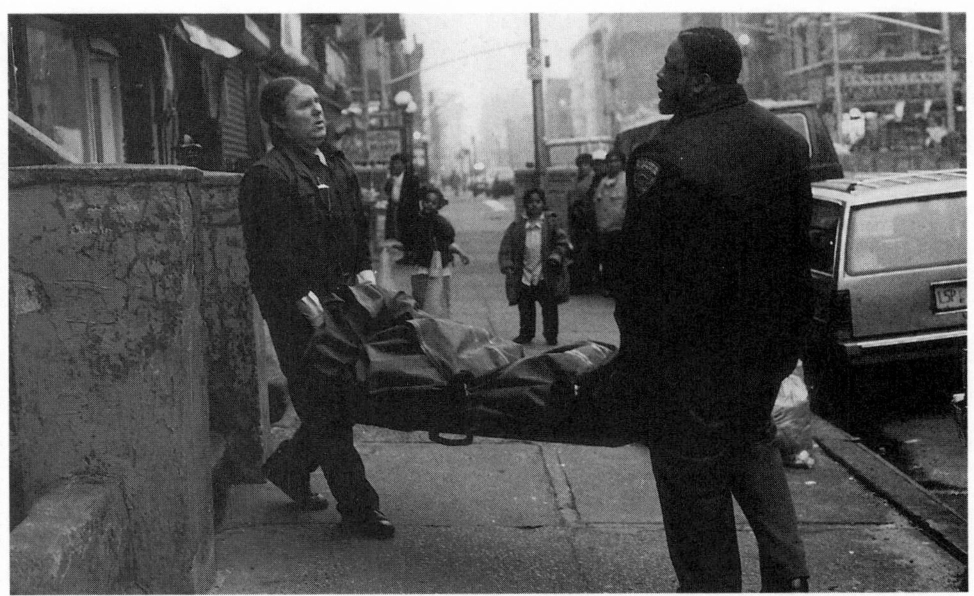

A dead body is removed from an apartment and sent to the morgue for examination.

was stretched as a result of his hanging there for a few days. But I try not to even remember these things. When they happen, they happen." He shrugs his shoulders and waves his hand for the check, adding, "But one that sticks out in my mind very clearly is a double homicide of a male and a female shot in a beauty salon. It was drug-related. It was pretty upsetting. You have to be tough to deal with it. Some cops still get queasy at the sight of blood." He sighs. "There are millions of horrors out there."

8:00 P.M.

Finished with his meal, Mayfield leaves the restaurant and crosses back under the elevated tracks of the subway, which runs aboveground in this part of the city. He walks the pathways around the Dyckman Houses. He's patrolled these buildings for so many years, most people know him by name. He

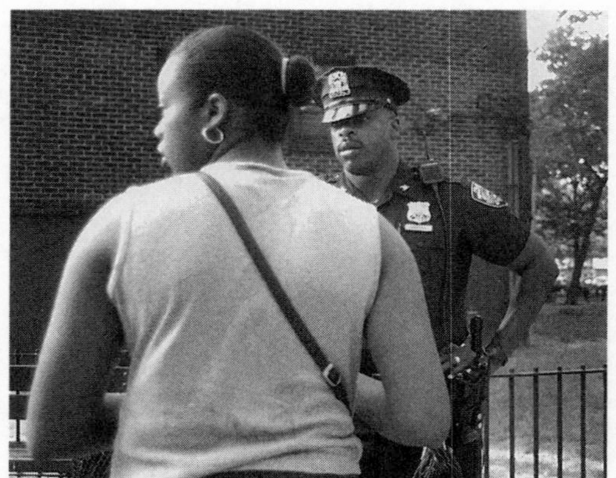

Officer Mayfield speaks with a resident of the Dyckman Houses.

knows them by name, too, and in some cases for all the wrong reasons.

"Hey, Mayfield." A young woman in a T-shirt and jeans waves a shy hello and walks over.

"Hey, how ya doing?" he asks, sounding concerned, his hand on his hip. "What's happening with the family? Is everything all right?"

"Yeah, everything's okay," the woman replies, looking away. "At least for the moment."

"Let's hope things stay calm. Make sure that you stay out of trouble," he advises.

"Okay," she replies, biting a nail and heading back to her parents' apartment.

Her older sister, Mayfield explains later, has been in trouble before, leaving her three children alone in the apartment, fighting with other women in her building, and lodging false complaints of abuse against different boyfriends.

"Under the law, these guys have to be locked up. She's using the system," Mayfield says. "She's even known by the district attorney's office for making these complaints. They have to investigate each guy after we arrest them. When we hear the address over the radio, we know it's her."

The young woman and her sister are just two of about five thousand tenants living in the Dyckman Houses. Built in 1951 on a plot of land that borders the Harlem River, the complex contains seven fourteen-story buildings, a total of 1,167 apartments, which are filled mostly with black, Puerto Rican, and Dominican neighbors. Over half of the residents are elderly or under the age of twenty-one. Mayfield pronounces it very safe. The Dyckman Houses have one of the lowest crime rates in New York City public housing.

"People hear 'New York' and they think high crime rates and it's got to be rough, that you've got to be really tough to survive. But New York is like any other place," explains Mayfield. "You have good sections and bad sections. Here in Washington Heights and Inwood, you've got certain areas that are more decent than other sections, where drug dealers and other criminals hang out."

Three residents of the Dyckman Houses pose for a photograph.

In the twelve years he's worked this beat, Mayfield has seen residents graduate from high school, marry, and have children. He's watched kids move from training wheels to the latest two-wheeler to Rollerblades, scooters, motorcycles, and cars. He's observed tenants moving in and moving out. And he's been called to the scene of these neighbors' accidents, injuries, heart attacks, and deaths. "I haven't had to deliver a baby—yet," he adds nervously.

Crime throughout the whole city has dropped. There were 672 murders in 2000 and 642 in 2001. Officer Mayfield can recall only three homicides at the Dyckman Houses in the last six years. The most recent one occurred on Mayfield's day off.

In May 2001, a twenty-year-old Dyckman resident killed a neighbor and later confessed to a previous killing in the same building. Mayfield read about the incident on the front pages of the newspapers the next day. The killer, a disturbed young man, said he wanted his victims' apartments. "I'm sure I've seen him before," Mayfield says. "You just never know what people are going to do, even in a pretty calm place like Dyckman."

The number-one reason for police calls at the Dyckman Houses and other neighborhoods in New York City is disputes. These can be fights between neighbors or fights between husbands and wives, arguing over money, children, belongings, pride, and other men and women. When one of the spouses or a concerned neighbor phones 911, Mayfield or another cop arrives to stop the fight and, if it has become violent, make an arrest.

"A lot of times I can understand because if I listen to the nature of the argument, sometimes it hits home. I may have been there myself in a relationship," Mayfield says patiently. "I may know what he's feeling. I may know what she's feeling. I don't go in there taking anybody's side. I say, 'Hey, listen, maybe you should do this or maybe you should do that.' Every dispute is not an arrest situation. The other thing you have to be concerned about is not assuming that the man is causing the trouble. How many times have you seen a domestic situation and the guy comes out in handcuffs instead of the woman?" he asks. "It could be the woman. I separate them until I've got both sides of the story. If they're both wrong, then guess what? They both can go to jail that night."

When arriving at the scene of a dispute, Mayfield stands at the apartment door for a moment before knocking, listening to how far the disagreement has escalated. When he enters, he speaks directly and carefully without raising his voice. "You have to make sure it's safe to enter," he explains. "You don't know if he's got a gun or she's got a gun, or he's got a knife and she's got a knife."

A large percentage of the neighborhood population does not speak English. Mayfield has learned some Spanish, but often recruits neighbors to translate for minor complaints. For more serious situations, "I'll get a Spanish-speaking police officer," he says. "It's challenging but it can be frustrating," he admits of the language barrier. "Sometimes people demand to know how come I don't speak Spanish. Nothing frustrates me more than when someone tells me to speak Spanish when they don't speak English."

The second-most-common reason for 911 calls by residents of the Dyckman Houses is the need for medical help. The police are typically on hand

Officer Mayfield listens to his radio.

in serious medical emergencies in case paramedics need assistance in calming family members or restraining a crowd. A police officer will also make a report on the incident, which is crucial if the emergency turns out to have a criminal cause.

The third-most-common call is about criminal mischief, which is usually property damage—someone sticking glue in a door lock or breaking a window.

And after that, calls are typically complaints about quality of life. Quality-of-life issues include loud radios and dogs off their leashes.

"This place is paradise compared to others," Mayfield says, bending down to pick up a gum wrapper and placing it in a trash can.

Now, on his current spot on a path by the Dyckman Houses, Mayfield hears his quiet radio squawk to life. The dispatcher calls out, "Man with a gun, 187th Street and St. Nicholas Avenue. . ." Mayfield stops and listens: one of the most dangerous calls on the radio is the report of a person with a gun. The location is too far for him to walk or run. Other nearby officers answer the call and Mayfield waits to hear the outcome of the job.

"X-ray, Central," a patrol car radios in to the dispatcher, meaning they did not find a man with a gun at that location.

Mayfield explains that it could have been a false report—a cell phone may have been mistaken for a gun. Or a man with a gun may have been spotted, but he could have left the area before the cops arrived.

Sometimes people call cops to a scene to divert attention from illegal activity on another block. "We don't know if it's false until we get there. We have to be ready to deal with a gun," Mayfield says, making another loop around the Dyckman Houses and entering a building. He rides the elevator to the top floor and walks up the stairs to the roof for an aerial view of the neighborhood. He spots a patrol car speeding across Dyckman Street, its lights flashing on its way to another job.

12:00 P.M., THE NEXT DAY

Mayfield gets his assignments from the station house of the 34th Precinct, often referred to as "the precinct." He is just one of 203 cops with the rank of police officer who work out of this building on Broadway, seventeen blocks south of the Dyckman Houses. The police officers are supervised by higher-ranking cops—thirty sergeants, eight lieutenants, two captains, and one inspector. The faces and the numbers fluctuate, sometimes on a weekly basis, as a graduating class from the Police Academy adds a dozen new cops to the precinct, or a cop transfers or retires.

As a beat officer with the precinct's community policing unit, Mayfield is usually assigned to walk the Dyckman Houses, but there is no typical day for a cop in New York City. Mayfield may walk or ride his bicycle on his beat, be called to court, be deployed to another part of the city in an emergency, or ride in a patrol car as a substitute for an absent cop. "I love riding my bicycle. I love working by myself," he says enthusiastically. "I enjoy the monotony of working in a car sometimes. I like working parades and rallies."

Today he will walk his beat again, but this afternoon he begins his shift at the station house, in a cubicle he shares with Officer Wendy Staffieri. Sometimes he rides his bicycle with Staffieri by assignment or for company. She specializes in meetings with neighborhood residents and crime prevention surveys. They've known each other since they were rookies in the Police Academy and have an affectionate, humorous rapport.

"He's a perfectionist. He's very meticulous with his paperwork," Staffieri says while Mayfield reaches for a new summons book. Their cubicle is in the

Officer Mayfield and his colleague Officer Wendy Staffieri

rear of the building, in a far corner of a room that is sectioned off with wool-covered partitions. The air is stale with cigarette smoke and the overpowering scent of a male cop's cologne. "He hates to be wrong," she adds as Mayfield walks out of their cubicle to check his file cabinet. "He won't admit to being wrong. He'll go down fighting."

The two ride twenty-one-speed police bicycles. These are more sophisticated versions of the bikes police officers first used in 1895 when Police Commissioner Teddy Roosevelt, later president of the United States, formed a traffic patrol unit called the "Scorcher Squad." Bikes are a great way to get around in the city. They are faster than walking or running and are easy to maneuver through traffic or along pathways like those at the Dyckman Houses. And a cop on a fast bike often has the advantage of surprise.

Mayfield and Staffieri have been riding with cracked safety helmets, and Staffieri now assures Mayfield that she called to request new ones.

"When did you call?" asks Mayfield, throwing up his hands. "Wendy, you failed us!" he cries out.

"Oh, please," she throws back, pretending to ignore him. The new bicycle helmets have an all-weather brim; their old ones don't. "It's like asking for a bar of gold," she says.

"Out of my cubby, Staffieri!" Mayfield barks playfully, and sits down next to her desk with a Pepsi.

"Hey! This cubby belongs to the New York City Police Department!" she retorts.

Officer Mayfield at the scene of a dispute

Later, as Mayfield leaves the station house to head out on patrol, he praises Staffieri and adds, "I don't like working with everyone, but as a professional you have to put all your differences to the side. What you're out there doing comes first."

As Mayfield walks, his eyes scan Broadway for trouble—a person running, a suspicious bulge that might indicate a gun, a car without license plates, someone smoking marijuana, or congregations of people on corners.

"Three-four, sector David."

It's Mayfield's radio. The police dispatcher is calling for a patrol car in the precinct: "3-4" means the 34th and "sector David" means a particular section of the neighborhood. (Every neighborhood in the city is divided into sectors and assigned a patrol car.) The call is about a man with chest pains, possibly a heart attack. The dispatcher gives the address. Since Mayfield is just across the street from the building mentioned, he radios back that he will respond. A team of paramedics has already arrived on the scene, so Mayfield checks on the man's condition and leaves.

Moments later, another call comes in. This one is about a dispute two buildings away.

"When I show up at the scene of something, I pretty much like to take control," Mayfield says as he walks quickly to the address. "If a patrol car pulls up, I'll try to immediately let them know that I'm managing the situation. I've seen situations where cops show up at the scene with the wrong mentality or wrong approach. Just when you have things under control, they make matters worse," he explains. "I've worked with cops who are good. But I've worked with some other people I never want to work with again." He adds, "I'd really rather work by myself, so that way I can't be implicated or be accused of nothing by people angry at the other cops."

Mayfield arrives at the building of the dispute. The woman who phoned the police is waiting downstairs. "Mayfield, I'm having a problem with a neighbor," she complains. "She curses every time she sees me."

"Where is she now?" he asks, moving her away from the doorway.

"She went into her apartment," the woman replies.

He takes her aside. His advice: "Just ignore her. I know it's difficult, but don't get yourself into trouble."

Later he comments, "I consider myself to be a talker and I can talk my way out of most things and talk people into seeing the logical side of things most times. If talking is going to resolve it, then that's what you want to do before it escalates to anything else. I'm sure every police person in New York City could go out and find somebody to lock up every day, if they wanted to. There is always someone in violation of something, someone engaged in criminal acts. You can go out there and do that. But would you want to?" he asks. "One of the good things about my job is I use my own judgment, not somebody else's."

2:00 P.M.

As he walks on the paths of the Dyckman Houses, watching twin sisters in identical dresses stroll by munching from identical potato chip bags, Mayfield says, "Although I spend so much time dealing with the criminal element, it's refreshing to see the success stories. I love seeing kids in their graduation caps and gowns. On the other hand, you see kids taking a turn for the bad, strung out on drugs. It makes me feel old. Drugs are everywhere. We're combating the problem, but we'll really never get rid of it. But you can see that the quality of life has improved over the last few years."

The younger generation of the Dyckman Houses

As he walks briskly toward the entrance of one of the Dyckman buildings, a black woman in a purple pantsuit flies out the door and into Officer Mayfield. Her seventy-eight-year-old mother, suffering from Alzheimer's, wandered out of the apartment and is nowhere to be found. Mayfield escorts the concerned daughter back to her residence and begins the missing person process. First, he searches from room to room, under beds and in closets. He asks the daughter questions so he can make a detailed missing persons report: What was her mother wearing? What does she look like? Where are her medical and dental records? He obtains a photo of a pleasant-looking gray-haired woman, then leaves the apartment, saying with concern and confidence, "We'll do our best. Her description will go around the city. We'll find her."

On his way out, Mayfield walks the stairs on both sides of the building: she may be sitting on the steps. As he looks, he calls his supervisor on the radio with the details. His supervisor, a sergeant, will coordinate the missing-person search. The sergeant will have the missing woman's description broadcast over the police radio on the chance she might be spotted by a patrol car in another precinct. He will also order the seven buildings of the Dyckman Houses searched by several cops.

In the meantime, Mayfield heads back to the station house, where he telephones the Transit Police, who are alerted to check buses, subway trains, and platforms, and the Housing Police, who will look for her within other public housing developments around the city. Finally, he calls the headquarters of the New York City Police Department to talk to the Missing Persons Bureau, a central information center for all missing persons cases.

The frantic daughter calls the 34th Precinct every few minutes. Two hours later, the missing woman is spotted by cops in another precinct and taken to a local hospital to be examined for any cuts and bruises. "You just hope for the best," Mayfield says.

Officer Mayfield patrols stairwells in neighborhood buildings.

5:00 P.M.

Mayfield is back at the Dyckman Houses, continuing his beat. He kicks a rock out of the way on the cement walk and waves to a woman on the opposite path. The school year ends in two weeks and hot summer nights will attract more people outdoors. He spots another woman pushing a homemade wooden cart full of flavored ices up the path. No vendors—with or without licenses—are allowed on public housing property and he has warned her before. She looks at him as if he's not there, parks her cart, and starts selling her ices. If he doesn't ask her to move, then Elouise Whitehurst, the president of the Dyckman Houses Tenants' Association, will want to know why. The tenants' association is a group of residents who meet and take action on community issues. They want to keep the neighborhood safe, and free of vendors who clog their pathways.

"Miss!" Mayfield calls out to the woman. "You're not supposed to be here! I've warned you many times before. The next time you're getting a summons."

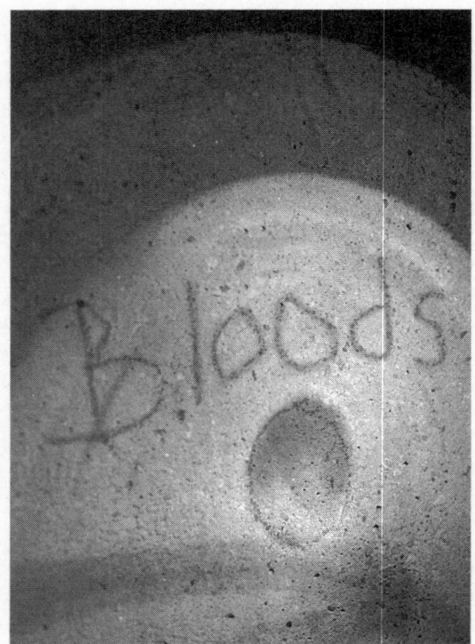

Gang graffiti is found in a stairwell in the Dyckman Houses.

She pushes her cart away and doesn't look back.

Now he heads inside again, shining his flashlight in stairwells to check for gang graffiti. He will report each sighting to a precinct cop who focuses on gang activity.

When Mayfield has a day off, other cops don't necessarily fill in on his beat. Or if they do, they may not be as familiar with the buildings and residents as he is.

"I can be out here breaking my back to improve quality-of-life issues, preventing graffiti or illegal peddling, but if other officers are not doing the same thing, these problems come back again," he says, frustrated. "They only seem to get enforced when I'm here. Some cops don't waste their time with them. But I understand the importance of quality-of-life issues, because I live in the city. It's a favorite cause of mine to enforce them. The bottom line is it improves life in the community and people appreciate it."

The housing complex is almost graffiti-free, which is unusual in a neighborhood where trees, rocks, mailboxes, walls, and cars are marred by spray paint. The lawns of the Dyckman Houses are neatly mowed and surrounded by wooden benches that serve as gathering places for senior citizens. In the northeast corner of the Dyckman Houses, a popular community center attracts kids, teenagers, and seniors for games, crafts, trips, lunches, and other activities.

Mayfield walks slowly through the winding paths around the center and notices two young boys cycling madly down one of them. They stop when they see him.

"Hey, slow down! Where's the fire?" he asks, smiling. "Just be careful." The boys nod shyly and continue on their way a little more slowly.

Mayfield greets a lively group of white-haired women, clutching canes and sunning themselves on benches.

"Hello, Mayfield!" they call out, almost together. "Nice to see you."

"How ya doing, ladies?" he calls back.

"Where ya been? We haven't seen you for a while," comments one lady, smoothing back her hair and sitting up a little straighter as he approaches.

"Well," he answers, removing his hat and rubbing his forehead; "I was working the midnight shift for a while. But now I'm back," he says brightly.

Officer Mayfield reminds two young Dyckman Houses residents to be careful while bicycling.

Mayfield reaches the community center, with its bright orange walls and bulletin boards filled with photos of neighbors. He sits down in the small office. Elouise Whitehurst, who is both the president of the tenants' association and chairperson of the board of directors of the community center, is talking on the telephone, so he waits for her to finish.

"Well, Mayfield, where've you been?" she asks, her voice indicating she means business. "We haven't seen you in a while. There's a lot of things that's been happening here."

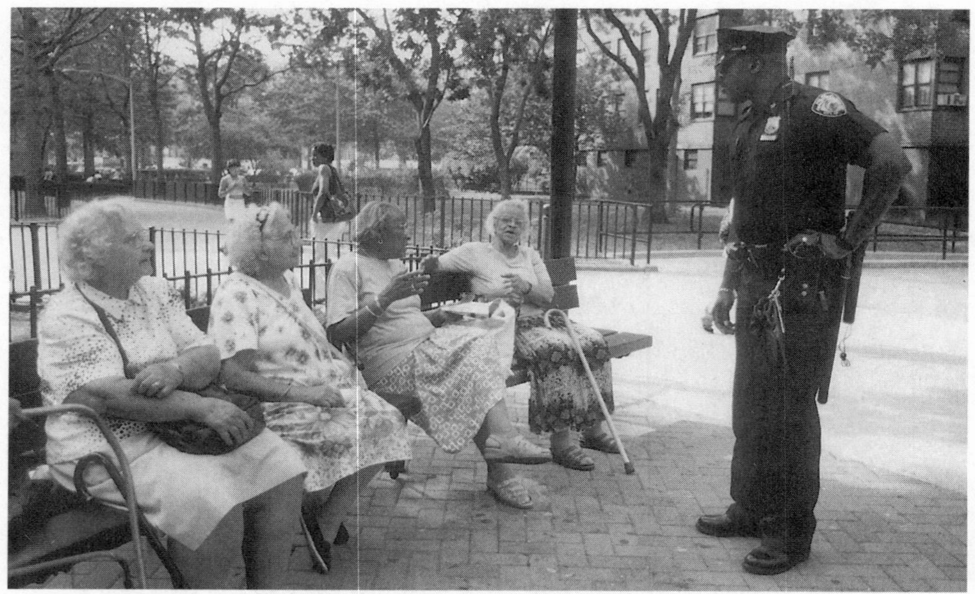

Officer Mayfield greets a group of seniors at the Dyckman Houses.

Mayfield takes off his hat and scratches his head. "They changed my hours," he says of the precinct, "so I was working the midnights. But, now," he declares, "I'm back."

"Good!" says Ms. Whitehurst. She is eighty-three and, as a girl, was one of the first residents of the Dyckman Houses. She's proud of her home. "I love the neighborhood and the accessibility to transportation. The buildings are nice and we get wonderful service. We don't have much crime. We don't have many muggings. We've had seven so far this year. That's quite a bit for the Dyckman Houses. We don't have rapes, murders, shootings. We have good, professional police coverage and concerned residents and tenant patrols. About 15 percent of the residents are involved in the tenants' association."

Mayfield stands up to greet a woman looking for Ms. Whitehurst.

"Hi, Steven!" she says brightly, holding a restless toddler by the hand. "How's your mother doing?"

"She's doing fine," he replies, a little embarrassed that his mother should be brought up. But the woman has been tugged away by her child and misses his reply.

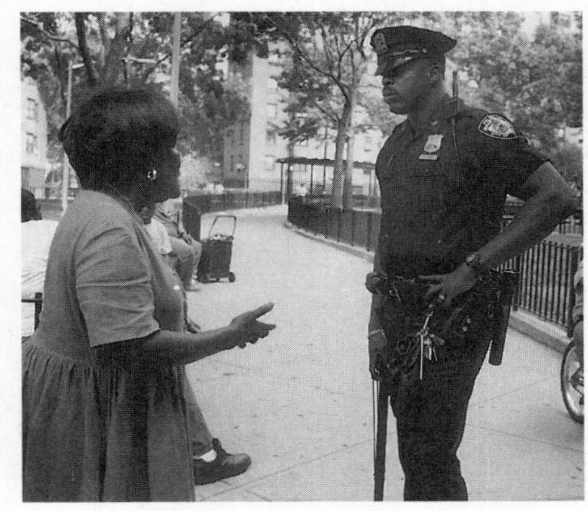

Officer Mayfield checks in with Elouise Whitehurst, the president of the Dyckman Houses Tenants' Association.

"Steven does his job well and in a professional manner," compliments Ms. Whitehurst. "He's not going to pull his gun and start running around. He has the respect of everyone. He's not lazy. Some cops see and don't see, hear and don't hear. He comes here or anywhere to do a job and he does it well. And we can tell when he's not here!"

Mayfield says good-bye to Ms. Whitehurst and decides to return to the 34th Precinct station house to pick up an extra summons book. "For a woman of her age," Mayfield says, "she gets a lot accomplished. Dyckman wouldn't be in the shape that it's in without her. She's constantly fighting for funding to get things."

As he walks he reflects on his part in keeping the Dyckman Houses safe, "Your obligation is to go out there and do your part. Nobody's asking you to go out there and run around like 'super cop' because you're not going to get paid extra for being super cop.

"The thing that you strive for is a good impression. I get people who walk up to me and I don't remember them from a can of paint. They say, 'Thank you for what you did. I bet you don't remember me.' They might refresh my

A young woman speaks with Officer Mayfield.

memory about something I did. And it could have been something small, something I did to help them along the way, whether it was advice or information or maybe getting them to the hospital . . . that's my job," he says.

"But people remember the small things. They appreciate them. It's a wonderful feeling when you stand on that street corner and that old man or that old lady walks up to you and says, 'Officer, it's a pleasure to see you here.' A lot of them don't understand how warm and how good a feeling it is for us to hear that from them. It don't have to necessarily be an old person. Anytime somebody welcomes you to their neighborhood and says, 'Thank you for being here, glad to see you here,' it's a pleasure."

But Mayfield's presence can also draw a different response; reactions of black residents to black cops are mixed. "Some look up to me respectfully," he says. "They feel I may better understand them than white cops. Others feel that I'm a sellout, keeping my own people down, and trying to impress whitey, that I'm working for the man. They don't see it as a job." He adds angrily, "The color of my skin isn't the issue, but they use it as an issue."

Blacks and Hispanics sometimes complain that they are unfairly singled out by cops in New York City. They make up more than 50 percent of the population so it *is* statistically more likely that a black or Hispanic person will be stopped by the police. It's also true that more victims of crimes are black and Hispanic than white.

"If I stop a person, I always let them know why I'm stopping them. I don't arbitrarily just stop people for the heck of it. If I stop you, I'll let you know why I'm stopping you," Mayfield says. "I like to put people at ease and let them know why I'm doing this. If I've got grounds to arrest, I do."

"Ninety percent of the time, bystanders have nothing constructive to say in an arrest situation. They might say, 'The only reason you're locking him up is because he's black or Hispanic.' A guy confronted me and said, 'You have something against minorities?' I said "What do you think *I* am?!' But I probably don't get as much attitude as a white officer would," he admits. "The public might be able to accept a situation better because a black or Hispanic cop arrives on the scene. People become more hostile when someone who is not a minority deals with them. They use it as an excuse. So you just have to do your best, maintain your cool, and just try to hold your head up when you're doing this.

"At Dyckman, I'm accepted as a black man and as a police officer," he says, shooing away a trio of teenagers sitting on the hood of a car with the car stereo blasting. "In other neighborhoods, the reaction to me is mixed. You don't have to like me, you have to respect me. Older people are happy to see the police. They remember how it used to be. They feel safe. But no young person ever told me that they were happy to see me."

A young Steven Mayfield

COPS AND ROBBERS

"Bang, bang!"

The boy presses the trigger of the black gun twice. Another small boy drops to the ground, clutching his chest. He lies still on the gray pavement with his eyes wide open. Rolling over, he picks up his gun and fires it at his friend.

"Bang, bang!"

When Steven Mayfield was young, he loved to play cops and robbers in the courtyard of the Jackie Robinson Houses, a public housing complex in East Harlem where he grew up. "I was always the cop," he says, "but maybe I was the robber, too. My mother didn't like toy guns in the house. She worried about us."

His mother still worries. "Police work? I don't care for it too much," Emma Mayfield admits. "It's kind of frightening with all that crime in the streets. I wasn't happy at all when he became a cop. But I never told him I wasn't happy. I used to worry like crazy. I used to watch the news and wait for the phone to ring, afraid something had happened to him."

Mrs. Mayfield, a soft-spoken woman with the same dark eyes as her son, describes Steven, the second youngest of her six children, as "always good." She continues, warming to the topic, "He was outstanding. I never had to track him down when he was younger. He was maybe a little quieter than the rest. I'm from the old school. I believe in bringing them up right. I tried to teach them to pick out the bad from the good."

Mrs. Emma Mayfield, Steven's mother

Her son says, "When I was in high school, I remember one morning making a pact with myself, saying that I would never do nothing to embarrass her."

Mrs. Mayfield has lived in the same three-bedroom apartment for over twenty-five years. She has watched her children and their friends grow up and have their own children. A whole wall of her home is covered with family photos.

"A lot of kids call me Nana," she says shyly. She sits under a sign in her kitchen that says FEELING LOW? NEED ADVICE? DIDN'T GET YOUR WAY? SHORT OF MONEY? CALL 1-800-GRANDMA.

She raised her children alone, working in a factory during the week and attending church every Sunday. Now Mrs. Mayfield works as a family assistant at a public high school in the Bronx, coordinating visits by social workers to students' homes.

She says of her East Harlem neighborhood, "It's gotten worse now. It changed with drugs." She looks over at two of her grandchildren who are watching television. "I'd like to take all the grandchildren to South Carolina and stay there until the summer is over."

She is the granddaughter of sharecroppers from the South. During the 1950s, her father headed to New York to work as a janitor, her mother as a housekeeper. It was a time when many blacks came from the Southern states to find jobs. Emma Mayfield arrived in New York at age eighteen. She has lived in the city ever since.

Steven Mayfield, who was born in September 1961, has the middle name Dietrich after his father, a man his mother never married. "I don't have very,

Mrs. Mayfield's wall of photos

very fond or very good memories about Mr. Dietrich," says Mayfield. "I knew him as Hanley Dietrich and not really remembering what type of work he did, but remembering that at some point in time he was out in Long Island. And that was basically it. Periodically, during the course of my life, I did see him. I think the last time I remember seeing him I might have been a freshman in high school. I certainly don't hold any animosity toward him. I can't be bitter because without him I wouldn't be here, so I guess I have to be grateful to that degree. But if he was to come forward, it would probably be a hard decision for me to accept him now, considering he hasn't been here all these years and now I'm grown and pretty much on my own.

"I guess," he admits, "I am bitter to some degree, but life goes on. I'm just fortunate that I've survived and been successful thus far." He adds, "I look at my mother. She's done a wonderful job and she's the father that I know.

And my brothers and sisters—if I did something wrong they chastised me, they straightened me out."

As a child, Steven Mayfield was industrious, filing papers in a neighbor's office and sweeping hair off the floor of Reverend Collier's Barbershop a few blocks away. In his free time, he loved watching the cartoon "Courageous Cat and Minute Mouse" and the television shows *Good Times, The Waltons, All in the Family,* and his favorite, *Little House on the Prairie.* "I loved that show," he says fondly. "It was so wholesome."

Young Steven Mayfield with Fresh Air Fund friends in Connecticut

Thursday nights were reserved for the cop show *Hill Street Blues.* "I liked it even before I was a cop," he recalls. "It seemed very realistic, and it got into the emotional aspect of the job."

For ten years, Mayfield was a Fresh Air Fund kid, leaving crowded East Harlem to spend summers in suburban Connecticut with the Harris family: J. T., Stevie, Johnnie, and their father, a postal worker, and mother, a nurse.

"I think it's a great program," he says. "It gives kids a ray of hope. I got a chance to see what life is like on the other side and to appreciate the suburbs." He and the three Harris boys learned to swim and ride bicycles. They attended day camp, glued arts-and-crafts projects together, hiked, and sometimes just sat by a pond, catching tadpoles.

"We ate breakfast, lunch, and dinner together every day. I have great, fond memories that I cherish," Mayfield recalls. "But I also remember very vividly the reactions we would sometimes get. The Harrises would take me out to restaurants where some people were not accustomed to seeing a black face.

Jim Harris had words with some people."

Sporting an Afro and plaid suits during the 1970s, Mayfield attended the Bronx's John F. Kennedy High School and joined the track team, running all year round.

"My special events were half mile and quarter mile. I was a high jumper, a long jumper, and a hurdler. Track was my outlet," he says. "Our track team was a very close-knit family. Irving Goldberg, the assistant principal, was like a father to us. I don't remember my grades being that great, but they had to be pretty decent for my mother to allow me to continue being on the track team, which was something I took very seriously.

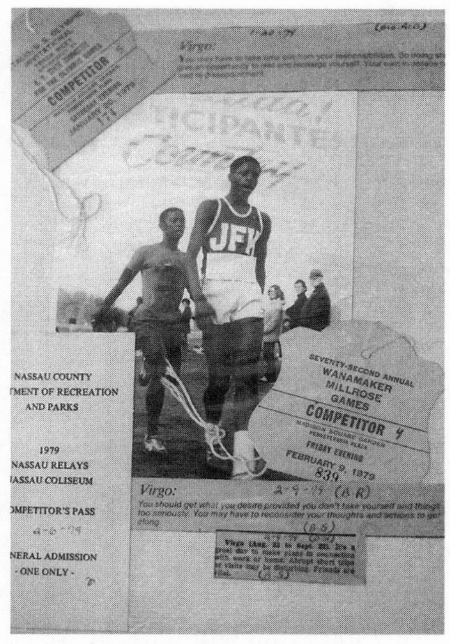

Young Mayfield at a track meet

"In fact," he admits, "I didn't even notice girls then because I was so heavily concentrated and focused on running track and field."

Walking to the subway one afternoon on his way home from a track meet, Mayfield spotted a man in his late thirties punching and slapping two young women in front of an apartment building.

"Nothing disturbs me more than seeing a guy beating up a girl," Mayfield says, still irate at the memory. He approached the man, stepping between him and the women."I said, 'Excuse me, sir, could I talk to you?'" Mayfield remembers. "I intervened because it was so wrong, and it bothered me. You can imagine how many people walked by and didn't say anything. And here I am, a junior in high school, and I walked up to the guy."

The man ignored Mayfield. "He was busy beating these two girls up. Then one girl picked up an empty bottle out of the garbage can. She said to him, 'If you hit my sister one more time, I'll bash you in your head.' I got kind of frustrated with the fact that this guy wasn't listening to me, and I didn't want to just jump in and grab him."

The teenage Mayfield looked at the girl holding the bottle and said, "If he hits your sister again, bash him in the head," then he walked away, hoping the guy would follow him.

Mayfield continues the story, observing, "So now he's got two choices. He can hit her and run the risk of getting bashed in the head, or he can go after me." The man accosted Mayfield, telling him to mind his own business. "I said, 'Sir, I just wanted to talk to you 'cause I thought what you were doing was wrong. Sir, I understand, it has nothing to do with me. I apologize, but I just didn't think it was right.'"

The man chased Mayfield with a pipe, enlisting friends to help. But Mayfield, with his experience as a runner, sprinted to the subway, where a police officer ensured that he got on the train safely.

The following Saturday, Mayfield noticed a man slapping a woman a few blocks from his home. Again, the sixteen-year-old intervened against a much older man, calling out "Sir, sir, why are you—? Don't do that, sir."

"The guy turned on me and so did the girl." Mayfield throws up his hands at the memory. "I said, 'Okay, I'm sorry,' and went about my business. But it's been my nature to get involved. I would hope somebody would help me under the same circumstances." He adds, "Now I get paid to do it. I always felt in my heart that I wanted to be in law enforcement. And being one of New York's finest was definitely my number-one goal."

Now, at Mayfield's Harlem apartment, a childhood friend remembers their old exploits. Harry Glenn and his family moved into the building next door to the Mayfields in 1973, and even though Mayfield is a New York Yankees fan and Glenn is a Mets fan, they became friends.

"We met playing basketball," Glenn recalls, careful not to mess up the pillows on the couch. Mayfield, as neat at home as he is in uniform, collects

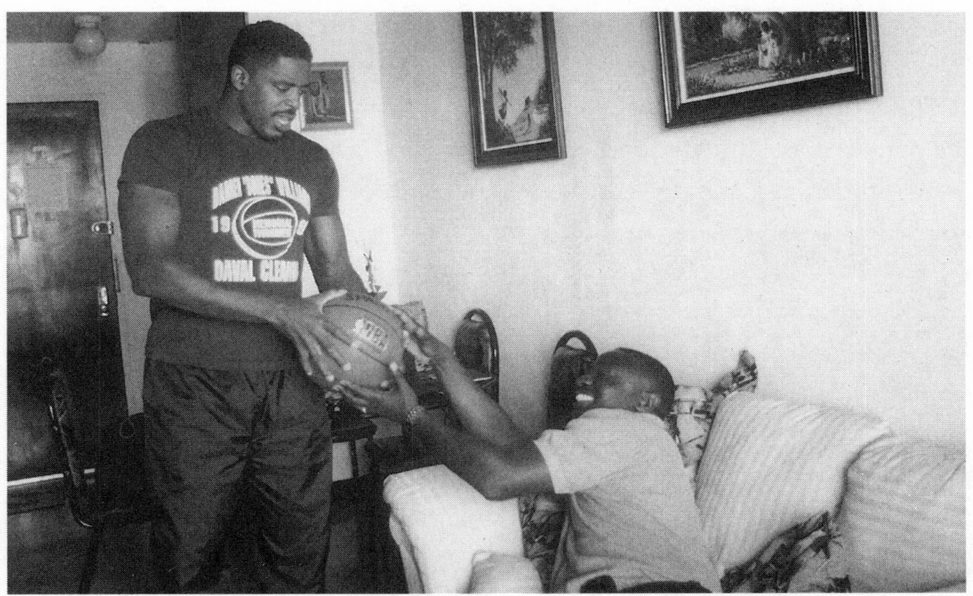

Mayfield and best friend Harry Glenn horse around.

a few errant crumbs from the floor with a carpet sweeper. As Glenn talks, Mayfield tightens the dripping cold-water faucet in the kitchen and wipes the kitchen table with a damp sponge. "We developed a camaraderie playing ball. Sports had a way of bringing us together. We competed pretty hard. We spent a lot of time at each other's house. And he does a great imitation of my father. 'Harry! Turn that music down.'" Glenn laughs. "We also spent some time dating or thinking about the same girls.

"We went through the puppy-love stage together, and when I was in the slumps with girls, I enjoyed seeing him making up or breaking up with some girlfriend.

"Neither of us had dates for the senior prom," Glenn admits as Mayfield laughs at the memory, "so we dressed up and went to see *The Muppet Movie* together."

Glenn also attended many of his friend's track meets, cheering Mayfield on. "I was never fleet of foot myself," he admits. "Steve was a lot more athletic."

The best friends shot hoops every chance they had, playing basketball on the neighborhood playground until it grew dark.

"We organized garbage-can basketball tournaments for the younger kids and fixed up our old trophies for them. I have a lot of good memories," Harry says, quiet for a moment.

A young Mayfield dressed to go out

"I'm not dead yet," interjects Mayfield.

These best friends separated when Glenn decided to attend college out of state, graduating from North Carolina Central University in Durham with a degree in business administration and computer systems.

"I wanted to leave New York," he says. "I wanted to go to a black college. We wrote to each other and worked together one summer at Lord & Taylor's department store. Holidays we always hooked up. He's family. At Christmas, Mother's Day, all the holidays, he shows up and everyone knows—there goes the food! And we would spend vacations trying to hook up with girls who dumped us. I guess we were lonely."

Glenn married in 1991, with Mayfield as the best man. He and his wife, Sharon, are the parents of a seven-year-old son. Now Glenn works in a Manhattan financial firm as a vice-president, specializing in computers.

After Mayfield graduated from high school, he enrolled at the State University of New York, where he majored in criminal justice, finishing his degree at

Mayfield's senior yearbook photo

the university's College of Technology in Utica.

Mayfield's decision to pursue a career in law enforcement didn't surprise Harry Glenn. "He was always the one who wanted to keep order. If he saw a guy picking on a little guy, he would step in." He adds, "I tip my hat to his patience. It's a stressful profession. Whenever you hear something happen to a police officer, I get a little concerned. It's a tough job."

Glenn tosses a basketball to Mayfield, who finally stops cleaning. He sits down next to his friend and reflects on his move from noisy New York City to quiet upstate Utica. "For the first couple of months, I had trouble sleeping 'cause I was so accustomed to hearing the traffic and the sirens. And the people upstate were so friendly and nice. I would walk down the street and strangers would blow their horns at me and wave. At first I was frightened," he admits. "But then I realized this is just how the people are!" He laughs. "I adjusted because I've always considered myself a country boy. I've always appreciated the country atmosphere—green grass, beautiful trees, peace, tranquillity, and quiet."

He lived in Utica for eight years, becoming the first member of his family to earn a college diploma, a bachelor's degree in criminal Justice.

As his first job after graduation, Mayfield ran a special program for delinquent children and teenagers at the Cosmopolitan Community Center in Utica. "A lot of these kids came from broken homes. There was no male role model. It was my first real job and I wouldn't have traded the experience for anything," he says fondly.

While working, Mayfield took civil service tests for corrections officer and New York City police officer and passed both. He expected to soon become a police officer, but during the required physical exam, the doctor detected a heart abnormality and pronounced him unfit to become a cop.

"I guess they felt that I was a risk factor; they thought I had a heart murmur," he says. He appealed, bringing in his own cardiologist, but he was turned down again.

"I became very discouraged," Mayfield says. "I had been set on being a New York City police officer since high school, when an Officer Loran came to talk to our class. Listening to him, I thought there was something about policing that sounded very adventurous and intriguing."

Mayfield continued to live and work in Utica, and one day he became a crime statistic himself. He was almost killed by opposing players during a local basketball tournament.

He remembers, "I thought the other team understood that when you're playing basketball, there's a lot of trash talking and when the game is over, it's over."

But two of the players, men in their late thirties or early forties, followed him after the game and started a fight.

"We were rolling around in a vacant lot, getting all cut up by bricks and glass. The sad thing about it is a lot of people were there—older people, too—who stood around and encouraged this conduct. I was petrified. I hit this guy with a right that was just picture-perfect and it staggered him," he recalls. "He dropped right to his knees like it was a boxing ring! You know, it was amazing! But I didn't want to fight this guy!" he protests. "I stopped, and I turned my back, and I walked away."

Mayfield returned to the park the following week to continue playing in the tournament. He thought the incident was forgotten. "I wasn't going to let this stop me, and I certainly wasn't going to let two guys dictate what I could and couldn't do," he says firmly.

Mayfield was standing on the court with his back toward the entrance. He didn't notice the two men from last week's fight walk onto the basketball court carrying baseball bats. Before he realized what was happening, one of them swung a bat at his head. It connected with a sickening thud.

"Everything just seemed like it was spinning. I could hear people screaming," he says. "But I still didn't know what was happening. I don't remember feeling any pain. It wasn't until the second guy swung and hit me in the hip that I went down."

Mayfield was rushed to the hospital, where doctors discovered his skull was fractured. "The hardest thing I had to do was to phone my mother. That shook her up, and she jumped on a plane and was out there. I tried to tell her, 'Nah, I'll be okay,' but you can't tell your mother nothing like that," he says, running his hand over a scar on the back of his head.

When Mayfield's two assailants went on trial, they were allowed to plea-bargain. "One guy received five years' probation and the other guy got six months at the county jail. He served maybe a month and a half or two months and they released him," Mayfield recalls with disgust. "The prosecutor says to me, 'Listen, you got the best deal you're gonna get.' And I say to him, 'Who the fuck are you to tell me this is the best that I can get? These guys almost killed me!' And he tries to tell me that one of the reasons they allowed the plea bargain was because I didn't die!"

The incident left Mayfield uncertain about his future, questioning whether a career in law enforcement was really for him. "I had lost all faith in the justice system. I said to myself, Why should I pursue a career in a system that is so unfair?"

But he reconsidered. "It wasn't the arrest that was unfair, it was the judicial system. I had lost all my faith in that system and I still don't have a lot of faith in it. I'm grateful and thankful that I survived, that I lived to tell about it. But it set me back psychologically. I didn't believe this could happen to me."

Mayfield (back row, fourth from left) and other corrections officers

Mayfield considered retaliating against his assailants, as some people might have done, but realized, "There are things that you can't change. These were two guys who had nothing going for themselves and never would have anything going for themselves. It wasn't worth it."

Mayfield recovered and returned to his job working with teenagers. Not long after, the New York State Corrections Department contacted him. "They gave me a physical and detected the same heart problem the New York City Police Department doctor did. But when they had a second doctor review the tests, I passed," he recalls. "I started preparing myself for a twenty-five-year career in corrections."

He worked for three and a half years at Sing Sing Prison in upstate New York. "That was a great experience," he enthuses. "I'm just happy that I had

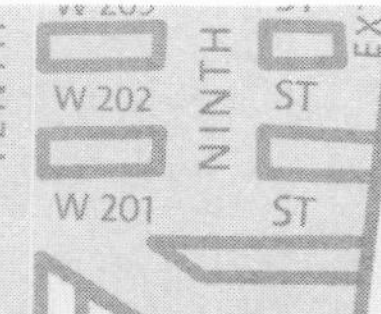

the opportunity to do that, because it helped me grow and learn how to deal with people."

Sing Sing, a medium- and maximum-security prison holding approximately 2,500 inmates, is the oldest jail in New York State. Every cell is locked manually, unlike in more modern prisons, where a lever closes or opens an entire row. Mayfield worked in the maximum-security area of the prison, where the most serious offenders are kept.

"The reason I was so fascinated is that you're dealing with 2,500 different people with 2,500 different personalities. Everybody comes at you from a different angle," he says. "And one of the key things I learned is that most of these guys had twenty-four hours a day, seven days a week, 365 days a year to sit in their cells and think of something to say to me that was either disrespectful or an attempt to convince me to do something for them that I wasn't supposed to, like bring them a weapon or a sandwich—something they had a craving for. There was one guard who was bringing in switchblades. And the sad part is," he continues, "I don't know how much he was getting for them. I really feel that there is not enough money that anyone could offer me to bring in a switchblade. What the other guard failed to realize was that not only was he jeopardizing the lives of other corrections officers, but he was jeopardizing his own life. What was to prevent a prisoner from using it against him? This guy brought in several of them before he was caught. I'm straight by the book. This is the way it's going to be."

Mayfield hates the word *guard,* his title while he worked in corrections. "Just the sound of it . . ." he says. "It sounds so harsh.

"One of the things that I really found intriguing is after being there for so long, you bond to some degree with these inmates. I always took into account that they're human beings who made mistakes," he notes. "I used to enjoy having conversations with these guys because most of the talks were interesting. But then there was always the point when they started placing the blame

on people other than themselves. I can't remember too many guys saying 'Yeah, I was guilty of what I did.' I would have to cut conversations short because it always came down to the white man: the white man was responsible for them being there. And with no hesitation I would say, 'Listen, I don't mind conversating with you, but when you start getting into that revolutionary bullshit, I have no desire to talk to you anymore. When are you going to start accepting responsibility for your own doing, because the white man didn't make you sell drugs, the white man didn't put the gun in your hand and tell you to pull the trigger. These are decisions that *you* made.' So that was one of the things that I always expressed to them, that a lot of them would not own up to the fact that they did something wrong."

Because of his large physique, Mayfield found himself challenged by prisoners more often than his shorter and lighter counterparts. Unlike police officers, prison guards don't carry guns, just batons. This was Mayfield's only protection in a housing block that was home to seven hundred inmates.

"Most people look at me and say, 'A guy of your stature, I know you didn't have any problems.' And that's one of the biggest misconceptions about prison," he explains. "What I learned is, the bigger you are, the more people are going to challenge you to prove how tough they are. So it is completely opposite of what people think. Sometimes the biggest prisoners were not the toughest. It's the short, wiry guys who had more to prove than the big guys. Small people always feel that they have more to prove than big people.

"I had another weapon that was stronger than a baton. And that was the mighty pen," he adds, pretending to write. "Everything is pretty much done on a merit system. If you get an inmate who picks a fight, you put that inmate on paper by writing up a violation. He runs the risk of being locked in his cell for twenty-three hours a day. He's entitled to come out for just one hour of recreation. A lot of them did not want to be faced with that. So if you used your pen the right way, you gained a lot of respect."

Mayfield's responsibilities ranged from supervising inmates to strip-

searching new arrivals to policing the Kool-Aid to ensure that each man received his ration.

At night or when there was a head count, every inmate was required to lock himself into his cell. "I'd call out, 'Okay, everybody find your house,'" Mayfield recounts. "'Lock into your house.' And every now and then you would get one of those wiseguys who would say to me, 'My house is in Brooklyn, I lock in Brooklyn.' I would say to him, 'Well, if you can't get to Brooklyn right now, then find your temporary home.' And that worked.

"Various guys would challenge and threaten you. Guys would say to me, 'Mayfield, I better not ever see you on the outside.' And I would say to them, 'When are you getting out, 'cause I'll meet you at the train station if you want to rock-'n-roll.' In other words, I would call their bluff. But you can't let your ego get in the way because sometimes you might find yourself in a situation where you can get hurt or cause your colleagues to get hurt if you react the wrong way," he explains.

"When I had to train new officers," Mayfield recalls, "I said, 'Understand something, these guys here in prison might be considered the bad guys. That's why they're here. But don't forget the fact that they're human, they are men. And for the most part, if you treat them with some respect, they won't be disrespectful to you.'

"I would add, 'If you're not scared or nervous about working in this environment, you need your head examined! You have every right to be fearful because some of these people are doing life, and some double and triple life. What do they have to lose if they killed you and me? Absolutely, positively nothing," he says. "I said it was like that deodorant commercial. You never let them see you sweat because most of them are just as scared as you are. You have to always be in control of the situation. There's something about prison that a lot of people fail to understand, the realities of the things that happen behind the walls, guys getting stabbed, guys getting killed, guys getting raped. That stuff is a reality."

Mayfield earned the nicknames Robo Cop and G.I. Joe. "Everybody knew me, the way I conducted myself, the way I carried myself. My uniform always looked sharp. I always had my hat on. It was something about the way I wore my hat that was very intimidating to a lot of people. It takes a tough person mentally to endure and deal with all the personalities and attitudes behind those walls," he says. "When you walk into a prison, when you hear those gates lock, you're an inmate also. The only difference is you go home at the end of the night, if all goes well."

Officer Mayfield in his police dress uniform at the 34th Precinct

Though he loved his job at Sing Sing, Mayfield still wanted to be a New York City police officer. So at the age of twenty-nine, he took the police written exam a second time and underwent another physical. This time the doctor did not detect an irregular heartbeat. The call came in October 1990: Was Mayfield still interested in becoming a police officer?

"And I said, 'Hell, yeah!" he exclaims. "I jumped at the opportunity. This was a dream, something I wanted to do all my life. I can't explain how excited I was. I felt here is a good job where I can help people, and fight the bad guys, and put the bad guys away!"

Harry Glenn smiles, remembering his best friend's decision. They now leave Mayfield's neat apartment for a spirited game of basketball at their old court. The taller Mayfield tosses a few in effortlessly as the sprightly Glenn jostles and jokes about his age. The old friends part about an hour later, promising

Harry Glenn and Steven Mayfield play a pickup game of basketball.

to speak again soon, and walk to their mothers' apartments in neighboring buildings.

At his mother's house, Mayfield devours his favorite dish, macaroni and cheese, fresh out of the oven, as Mrs. Mayfield recalls not being too happy about her son's decision to become a New York City police officer. "I was so nervous," she says quietly, clasping her hands and looking out of her kitchen window. "I never liked that gun. I said, 'Take it off, put it away. They're too many small kids around here. Unload it.' And I'm scared for him. I pray for his safety."

Officer Steven Mayfield and his partner for the evening, Gus Blain, in their patrol car

3

THE 34TH PRECINCT

ON PATROL

It is another sweltering summer evening in Washington Heights. After a swollen orange sun sets behind the buildings, the air is still warm and sticky, so heavy you can almost chew it. Heat feels embedded in concrete sidewalks. Neighborhood dogs, pit bulls and terriers, wince and whimper as their paws touch the pavement. T-shirts and sheets hang limp on clotheslines, but little kids, seemingly impervious to the temperature, blissfully swing around corners on their bicycles. Adults sit on beach chairs, gossiping and fanning themselves with newspapers while teenagers cluster on car trunks, listening to radios. It's hot, but cooler than in cramped apartments, so life has moved outdoors for the evening.

Men sitting on milk crates play intense games of dominoes, the tiles arranged on pieces of discarded cardboard they balance on their laps. Young men drive past with radios blasting, hoping to attract the attention of the groups of pretty women walking by in shorts and tank tops. Elderly men and women fan themselves on park benches. Commuters walk home from train stations—factory workers, mechanics, teachers and students, chefs and dishwashers, lawyers and secretaries, actors and actresses, writers and photographers are illuminated by streetlights and neon signs advertising pizza, Big Macs, vacations to the Caribbean, and malt liquor.

Police Officer Steven Mayfield, off his beat for the evening, looks at these vibrant streets through the window of a blue-and-white patrol car. Gus Blain, his partner for this assignment, slowly drives up Broadway, the main avenue here at the northern tip of Manhattan. The two cops work together when other officers are off duty and a patrol car needs to be filled.

Their windows are rolled up so the car's air conditioning can cool them in what will be their office on wheels for the next eight and a half hours. But the blasts of cold air cannot dispel the foul smell of Blain's endless cigarettes. Mayfield brushes an errant ash from his neatly pressed blue pants and grimaces.

Officer Gus Blain

"Do you have to smoke those things?" he asks as Blain lights up another cigarette.

"Yeah. And what are you going to do about it?" Blain retorts good-naturedly.

The Cuban-born Blain is a good match for Mayfield. Raised in Washington Heights, Blain speaks Spanish and knows the streets intimately. He likes to drive, which Mayfield doesn't, and he doesn't like handling their paperwork, which Mayfield does. Both have dark mustaches; eat bacon, lettuce, and tomato sandwiches for breakfast; and dislike coworkers they perceive as being uncaring police officers.

"I've come across people that I wouldn't want to work with again," Mayfield explained earlier. "Gus knows his work. He knows when to be aggressive and when not to be. These things are important. Our personalities clash to some degree, but we understand each other and we make the most of it. Sometimes we clash just to clash, for the heck of it. I think he gets a kick out of harassing me every opportunity he gets. But it's all done in fun. Otherwise we wouldn't work with each other. He's a good guy. I like working with Gus." He sighs. "Even with the smoking."

Officers Mayfield and Blain enjoy working together.

On this evening, they are assigned to look for stolen cars. Precinct statistics have indicated that they are being stolen on an average of one a day from the streets of Washington Heights and Inwood. Blain lights another cigarette and looks warily out the window. His lighter clicks in the dark and he begins to speak. Mayfield holds out his hand to silence his partner and puts his police radio up against his ear. "I think this is us," he says softly.

"Ten-59," the voice of the female dispatcher calls out to the 34th Precinct cops; it's the code for fire. She gives the address: "297 Wadsworth Avenue."

"Ten-4," Mayfield replies, indicating that they are responding to the job. He pushes the buttons on the dashboard that turn on their flashing lights and loud sirens. Blain steps lightly on the brake pedal, checks for traffic, then speeds through the intersection.

All the two men know is that someone has called 911. They don't know how serious the fire is, if anyone is badly burned or dead, if anyone is trapped inside an apartment, or even if the fire was set to conceal evidence of a crime.

From two blocks away, they smell smoke and spot the red glow of flames against the dark, hazy sky. Two fire trucks, their sirens blaring, race past them. Firefighters jump out as soon as the trucks stop, carrying hoses and wearing oxygen masks and tanks.

Mayfield and Blain pull up. They hop out of their car, slamming the doors, and stare up at the burning apartment. The firefighters will handle the fire; paramedics, also summoned via radio, will tend to the injured. Mayfield and Blain are responsible for crowd control. Curious and concerned neighbors and relatives have gathered outside the building and need to be kept at a safe distance. The officers can also help evacuate people if it isn't too dangerous to do so without fire gear.

Most of the block is watching as women in nightgowns, clutching small children, climb slowly and carefully down the steps of the fire escapes. Families stream out of the building entrance, too, as the firefighters break down apartment doors and smash windows to get at the fire and anyone still inside. Flames scorch bricks and smoke burns in the throats of the bystanders as they watch the hoses pump hundreds of gallons of water into the burning apartments.

Several stories off the ground, frightened women and children stand paralyzed on the old metal fire escape. They cannot move the heavy access ladder so it reaches the ground. A girl's doll falls and hits the pavement with a soft thud. Another girl of about fourteen or fifteen leans over the railing, her hair streaming and her face caked with soot, and waves frantically to Mayfield.

"Do something!" she screams, pointing to the ladder.

Mayfield swings into action. Tall as he is, he still stands several feet below the access ladder. He jumps and grabs the bottom rung and easily pulls himself up onto the fire escape. He reaches the first platform and lifts the rusted catch that holds the ladder in place, then pushes the ladder down so it reaches the ground. Blain catches and holds the other end in place.

"This way, ma'am," Mayfield says, ushering the women down the ladder as Blain meets them at the bottom.

Mayfield climbs back down the ladder. He and Blain stride to the front of the building to keep tenants from entering until they are sure it is safe. Firefighters finally douse the flames.

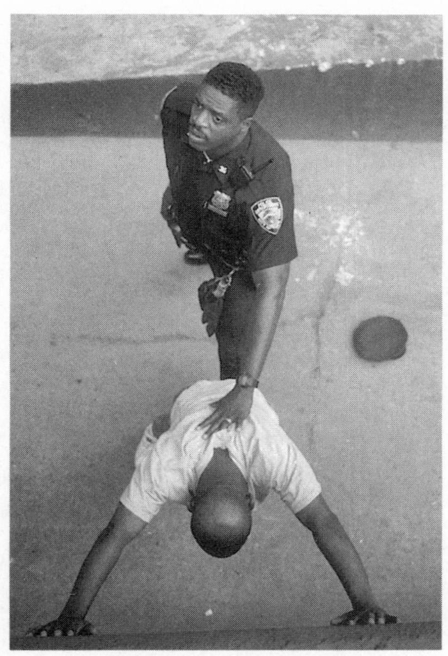
Officer Mayfield demonstrates the arrest of a suspect.

One woman can't find her mother. She stands in front of the building, screaming, *"Mamá! Dónde esta mi madre?* (Where is my mother?)" Mayfield, who understands some Spanish, assures her that he will try to locate her mother. He talks to one of his supervisors, a sergeant, who says that no one perished in the fire. Mayfield walks to the other side of the building and finds an anxious woman searching for her daughter. He reunites the two and watches as they hug each other tightly.

"I was relieved that everyone was okay," Mayfield says later. "It would have been a real tragedy if someone had died."

He dismisses his actions as those of a police officer just doing his job. "Cops encounter a lot of danger. Suddenly you find yourself springing into action," he adds. "You're so eager sometimes that you forget about the danger. You're often in a bad situation."

In twelve years on the force, he's encountered many bad situations. He's arrested more than one hundred men, women, and children. He's climbed through stairwells full of smoke, wrestled with drunks, and dealt with wife beaters and sellers of marijuana, cocaine, crack, and heroin. He has called for ambulances for people who were run over by cars, hit by pool cues, stabbed, or shot. The youngest person Mayfield arrested was a twelve-year-old girl who had slashed a boy in the face with a box cutter. The boy was trying to break up a fight and ended up needing one hundred stitches.

"At first, I was surprised to see how people live and treat each other. I don't put nothing past people," Mayfield insists. And when Mayfield started on the force in the early 1990s, the neighborhood of Washington Heights was at its worst.

THE DRUG WARS

In those days, the streets of northern Manhattan were so dangerous that gunshots were heard more often than the bells of ice-cream trucks. Young men hustled drugs on street corners, their customers double-parked in cars with license plates from New Jersey, Connecticut, and New York. Dead or nearly dead drug dealers and buyers were discovered almost every night. Washington Heights' open air drug market was so infamous that two highly placed government officials used it as the site of an undercover stunt meant to draw attention to the city's drug problem. Rudolph Giuliani (then the U.S. district attorney in Manhattan, later the city's mayor) and then-Senator Alfonse D'Amato, both dressed in casual clothes, were able to purchase crack cocaine, a highly potent drug, off a street corner in Washington Heights.

The overworked 34th Precinct, which then stretched from 155th Street to 220th Street, tried to combat the drug trade. Heroin was being sold in the south end of the neighborhood, while cocaine, crack, and marijuana were dealt at the middle and northern end. Dealers hid cocaine and crack behind billboards and storefront gates, in mailboxes and in holes in the sidewalk, anywhere they could be concealed from the police. Arresting people with drugs and guns became an endless task. And the drugs were still there.

From 1985 through 1993, Washington Heights was the hub of the New York City cocaine trade. Drug dealers with names like Chi Chi, Ace, Hippo,

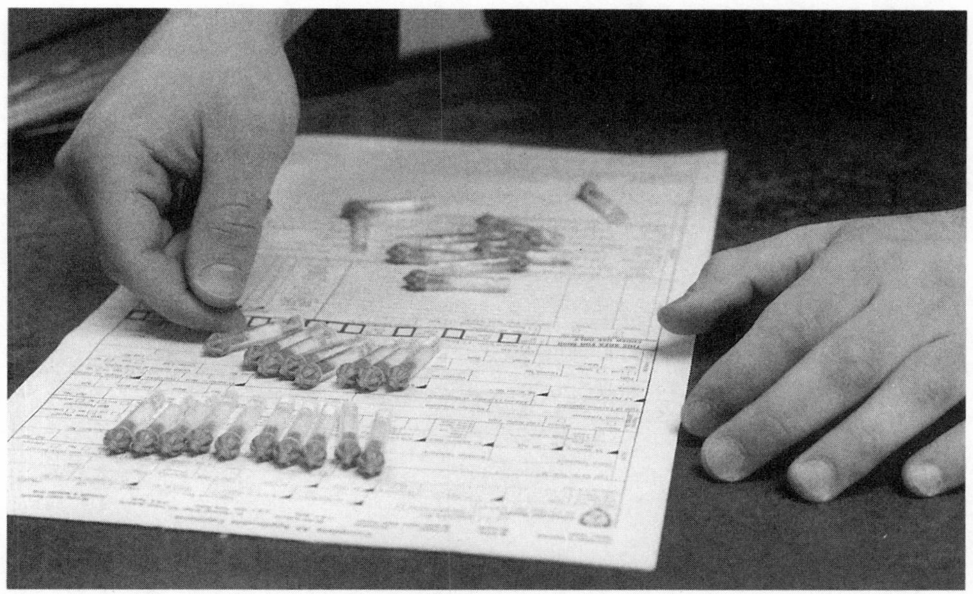

A police officer counts crack vials carried by a suspect.

Yayo, Macho, and Fresh ruled the streets. Law enforcement officials estimated that Dominican drug traffickers in the neighborhood transported one-third of the estimated three hundred tons of cocaine entering the United States every year. Local teenagers jumped at the chance to earn $2,000 a week delivering drugs.

This small percentage of residents terrorized the majority of the community. Residents not involved in the drug business suffered. Their children were not allowed to play outside because of the violence. And they were afraid to report drug dealers to the cops. One woman's twelve-year-old son was killed because he had been a witness to his father's murder at the hands of drug dealers.

A police officer from the 34th Precinct also became a casualty. Michael Buczek, a highly regarded officer with over thirty commendations, was shot

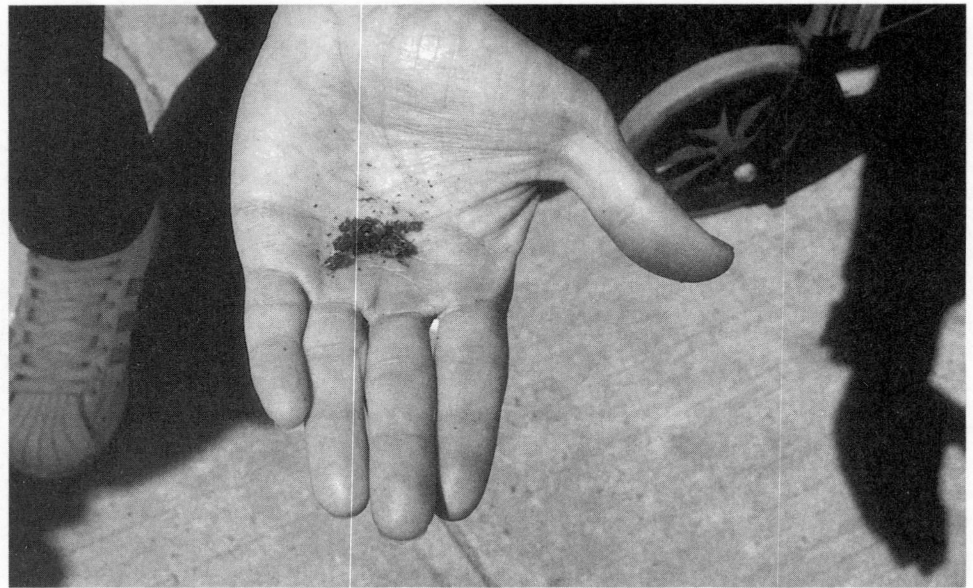

A police officer holds a small portion of marijuana leaves confiscated in a drug bust.

and killed in 1988 by a suspected drug dealer whom he and his partner were chasing. At that time, bulletproof vests were optional for cops; and Officer Buczek was not wearing one. That very same night Chris Hoban, an undercover cop from the narcotics unit, was shot and killed during a "buy and bust" drug operation in Harlem. He was not wearing a vest either. It was unprecedented: two city cops killed on the same night in unrelated shootings. As a result of their deaths, the police commissioner made wearing bulletproof vests mandatory.

The New York City Police Department intensified the war against the drug trade, adding special units of cops and undercover officers to deal solely with the drug problem in the neighborhood. More buy-and-bust operations were added, which meant more buyers and sellers of drugs were arrested.

The community and cops were headed for a confrontation. In 1992, Police

Officer Michael O'Keefe entered the lobby of a building on West 162nd Street, a known drug location to police. Officer O'Keefe said that he noticed a bulge in drug dealer Kiko García's waistband, which could mean that García was carrying a gun. García, with one drug-related conviction on his record, tried to run away and then attacked the police officer before taking out a .38-caliber gun. The two men struggled. O'Keefe fired his gun twice, hitting García in the stomach and in the back, killing him. Two women testified that Officer O'Keefe beat García with a police radio in an unprovoked attack and shot him to death. After an extensive investigation, the Manhattan district attorney's office determined they had lied.

Officer Mayfield puts on a bulletproof vest as he dresses for work in the 34th Precinct locker room.

Before the facts were out, the incident set off six days of disturbances, mostly by a small group of angry Dominicans, cops said, who wanted to remove police attention from Washington Heights so they could continue their drug business. Other Dominicans saw García as one of their own, wrongfully killed, who was just selling drugs to get by.

The violence ranged from West 125th Street in Harlem to West 204th Street. Stores were looted. Demonstrators threw bottles and rocks, overturned garbage containers, and taunted and fired shots at police officers. At one point, the rioters rushed toward the George Washington Bridge, an enormous structure that connects upper Manhattan to New Jersey, in an attempt to close it down, but they were prevented by dozens of police officers in riot gear.

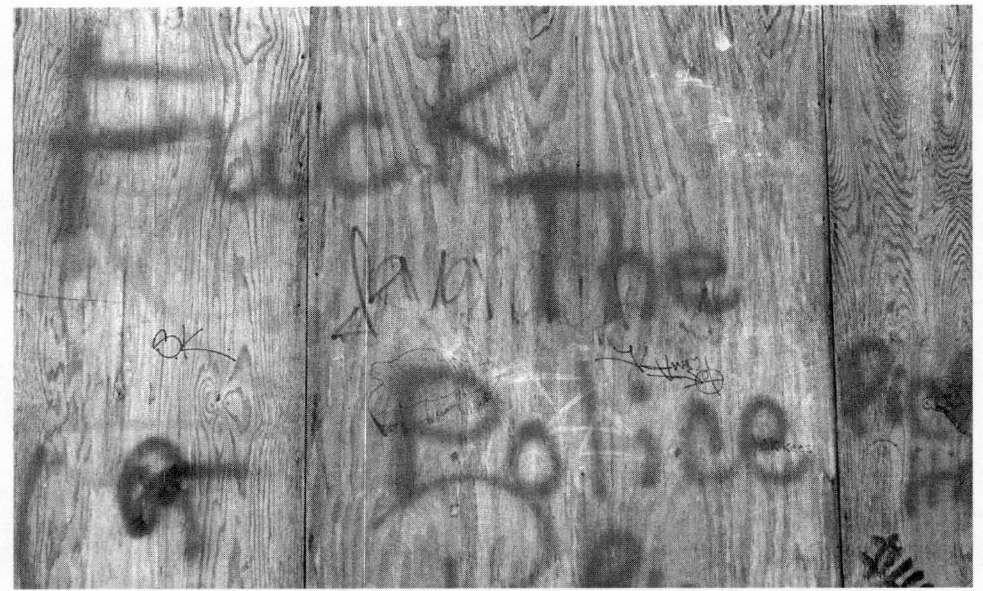

Not everyone is happy to see the police.

When the riots were over, there was one dead, ninety injured (including seventy-four police officers), one hundred arrests, fourteen burned buildings, and 121 vehicles damaged or destroyed.

"I wasn't frightened," says Officer Mayfield, who was assigned to patrol one corner of the neighborhood. "But I was nervous a little bit," he admits. "There was disbelief in the station house. We had never seen anything like it and it was in our own backyard. It made me look at people differently. I couldn't believe that a community could react to such a massive degree. They caused damage to the very community that they live in. And no one took to the streets to apologize afterward."

"We were in a riot zone," recalls veteran cop Tom Kennedy, one of Mayfield's colleagues in the community policing unit. "So many people were looting. Bottles were hitting us from all sides of our van. We had the windows taped over. It was pretty scary," he admits. "The looters were drug dealers and neighborhood kids, about sixteen or seventeen years old. It was the people who were involved in drugs who were rioting. It wasn't your average person."

Many police officers, as they struggled to keep the peace, felt angry and demoralized. Mayor David Dinkins visited the home of García and invited his family to Gracie Mansion in an attempt to quell the disorder and keep peace with the Dominican community. The city paid for his funeral, which was taken by many cops as a show of support for García.

Officer Tom Kennedy

"A lot of police thought it was wrong. I thought it was a ploy to defuse potential unrest," Mayfield explains. "It sped things up and got it over with."

"The riots had a positive impact," says Dr. Silvio Torrés-Saillant, director of the Dominican Studies Institute at the City University of New York. "At least people came to terms with the Dominican community. The mayor came to the community and vowed to do what he could. There was recognition that there were social problems, overcrowding, and unemployment. The community started to see itself and the problems that it had to deal with."

After the riots, the 34th Precinct was split into two. It now covers the north side of 179th Street up to 220th Street, while the 33rd Precinct handles the south side of 179th Street down to 155th Street. In 1996, then-Police Commissioner Howard Safir organized a city, state, and federal task force that pooled intelligence data and responded to every reported drug incident in Washington Heights. Gradually, many dealers were taken off the streets.

IN THE HOUSE

The last names of the police officers of the 34th Precinct reflect their diverse backgrounds: DeStefano and Stefanovich, Meléndez, Trinidad, Goldstein, Levine, O'Conner, Kennedy, and even a Smith or two. Their first names are Tom, Sal, Steven, Stu, Bob, Danny, Doug, Dave, Wendy, Carol, Mark, Mike, Tony, Jim, Joe, Betty, and Mary. There is a cop named Charity and a rookie cop with the ironic last name of Kil (first name Chuck).

Officer Dave Lawrence

Mayfield has his own small group of trusted friends, including Police Officer Dave Lawrence, who says, "Steve is idealistic and the epitome of what a community policing officer should be. He patrols his area frequently and he's well-known by people in the community. He interacts well with children and he's always involved in community projects. He's very professional, very caring."

Mayfield, in turn, admires Lieutenant Jim Meléndez for his ironic sense of humor. "A sense of humor keeps you afloat *and* keeps you grounded," he says.

Mayfield also admires Lieutenant Stuart Levine, the administrative lieutenant, who is always busy with schedules, meetings, and paperwork, ranging from vacation requests to lightbulb orders. "He's very smart, very competent. He knows what to do in the best interest of everyone," Mayfield says.

His friendship with Officer Wendy Staffieri offers him a different perspective. "With Wendy, I see things from a female perspective. Men can get too caught up with their egos and macho-ness," he says. "Diversity is good because you have the benefit of different ages and different experiences. Some people may be more patient, others faster acting, more athletic, more humorous, or more knowledgeable."

Lieutenant James Meléndez

No one is a "typical" cop. One cop used to work as a salesman at Sears. Another reads *The Wall Street Journal* religiously. One man collects G.I. Joe dolls. One captain has his mother read over his police memos before he sends them out. One woman was once homeless and on public assistance. One man trains dogs and loves to talk about animal psychology. Another grieves over the death of his mother. One woman is married to a firefighter, another to a bus driver. One cop's wife is a schoolteacher, another is a corrections officer, and a third, a social worker. A male cop covered with tattoos loves to ride motorcycles. A few tinker with computers. One repairs air conditioners. Others play golf regularly on their days off. Some like to hunt and fish, while others work as pallbearers to supplement their income—thirty dollars per casket. One has an herb garden and spends vacations visiting other police departments around the country. Several have served in the military. A lieutenant makes stained-glass lamps, and a captain flies helicopters as an emergency-response volunteer. Some have bonds with their partners stronger than those with their husbands and wives.

A few live on nearby Long Island, some in New York City, others in the suburbs upstate. Two divorced men live together to save on the rent. And in the tradition of *The Odd Couple,* one complains about the other's slovenliness and

Officer Teddy Ahokas

permits him to use just one plate, cup, and fork in their apartment.

Some cops are wonderful storytellers, while others prefer not to discuss the battles they've been in. Some have been fired at and fired back. One of Mayfield's supervisors shot someone to death, a junkie at a doughnut shop in the Bronx who fired a .22-caliber gun at him.

Many don't seem as interested in their weapons as people outside the force might think. One captain picks up his .38 revolver, sitting on top of a pile of papers. "You know what this is?" he asks. "It's a paperweight. Never had to use it. I put it on in the morning and take it off at night."

These cops range in age from twenty-two to sixty-two. The oldest is Teddy Ahokas, known as "El Cigar" for the cigar that is usually rooted in his mouth. He is also known as "Grandpa" and "Father Time."

"Everyone I worked with retired. I got thirty-one years as a cop," he notes. "That's older than most of the rookies. It's different now. During the sixties, it was the time of radical groups who used violence to protest. They were just shooting at cops. All they knew was to hate a uniform."

Back then, he patrolled Washington Heights in a green-and-white Chevy with no air-conditioning. He observes, "Kids have always been hanging around. Years ago, I'd tell them, 'You've got to move,' and they all left. Now they don't move. They want to fight you."

Ahokas once shot a bank robber and earned a Combat Cross from the

Police Department. "He was hidden behind a low wall, and if I hadn't shot him, he would have killed a cop," he recalls. "It bothered me. But you really don't have time to think. It's chaos."

Thirty-eight-year-old Gus Blain, Mayfield's sometime partner, was born in Havana, Cuba, arriving in Washington Heights when he was thirteen. His father, a doctor, was forced to remain behind in Cuba by dictator Fidel Castro. Blain remembers that his father treated people who traveled many miles to see him and allowed patients to live in the top floor of their home until they became well again.

After leaving Cuba, Blain grew up on 188th Street and Wadsworth Terrace in the Heights. "I did not know English. It was horrible. A teacher told me, 'You're not going to do anything but sell drugs on the corner.' It was devastating," Blain recalls. He became an electrician, but his brother-in-law convinced him to become a cop. "I like excitement, the adrenaline. I like the rush once in a while," he says. "You don't get that when you're wiring buildings."

Blain was on the scene when a young man walking with his girlfriend and daughter on Nagle Avenue suddenly fired a gun into the air. He could have hit an innocent bystander through a window or when the bullet came down. Luckily, no one was hurt. "He said he just wanted to see if the gun was working," Blain recalls. "He said he bought it from some Mexican on 207th Street. It was a brand-new .357 Magnum. Then he said it fell out of his pocket and discharged into the air, but that's not what we saw. The neighborhood probably has the same amount of guns as it always has. Now they're just concealed better. Now they're fired on New Year's Eve, the Fourth of July, and on Halloween by people with masks on!"

Officer Mayfield speaks of the differences among his colleagues. "Some have an honest work ethic and some are counting down to their pensions," he says. "I can't sit back and work twenty years like that. I need something to motivate me and to keep me going. I need the excitement to some degree."

Cops are united by their feelings about public criticism and by complaints

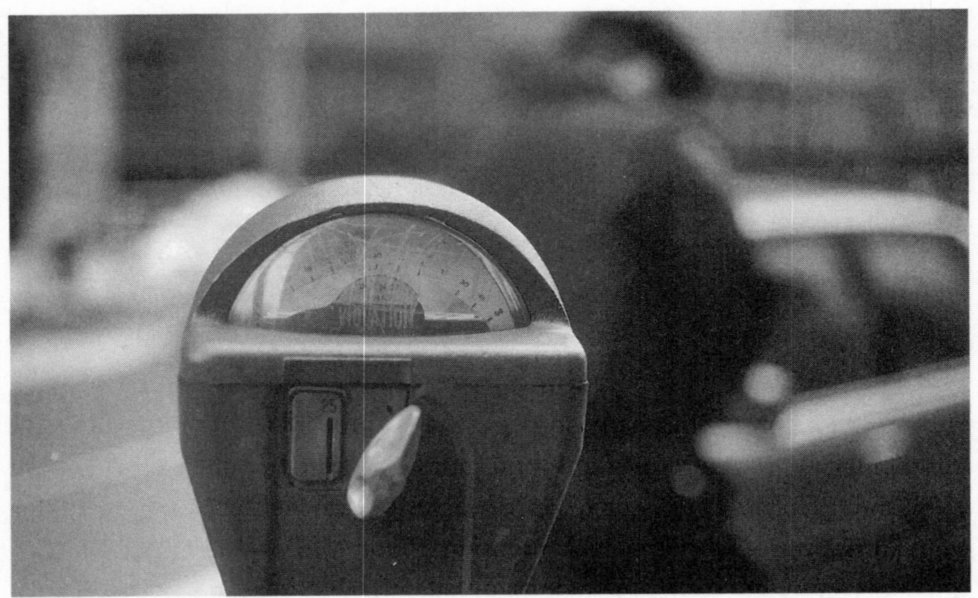

A police officer writes a parking summons for a car parked at an expired meter.

about low salaries. Every so often they will retaliate against the mayor or their commanding officer by not writing summonses, the traffic tickets that provide hundreds of thousands of dollars in income to the city of New York each year.

"When I was a rookie, I remember being confronted by veteran officers who saw me writing a parking summons," Mayfield says. "They said to me, 'What are you doing?' I said, 'What does it look like I'm doing? I'm writing a summons!' And they said, 'Don't you know we're in a slowdown?' I made them aware of the fact that they might be in a slowdown, but I was not," he protests.

"Politics inside the precinct can be draining," Mayfield adds. "There is the pressure to conform, and if someone doesn't, they may find their locker moved into the shower, carried there by cops sending a message."

As is the case in many occupations, if a cop knows someone, he or she may be placed in a desirable unit such as those specializing in organized crime, narcotics, or gangs. And as in almost every workplace, gossip and rumors abound, about who the next police commissioner will be, when the inspector will be replaced, which woman is single, which man complains the most, and everything else in between.

"I'm sure this is not an isolated thing. This happens in most of the precincts. I am aggravated by it," Mayfield says of the gossip. "You still have to maintain your professionalism. I can't allow myself to get aggravated within the precinct and then go take it out on the public. It's not fair. But the city don't pay me to take garbage from both inside the precinct and outside on the street. We are all supposed to be on the same team."

The 34th Precinct

The cops of the 34th Precinct work together out of a station house that looks as if it were built backward on Broadway. Three seldom-used garages sit in the back, too close to a brick wall to allow easy access.

Inside, there is a waiting area, with benches made of stainless steel that look like tables from the morgue, and a muster room that has vending machines for soda, ice cream, and candy. This is where cops stand in uniform for roll call and receive their assignments. Decorating the main area outside of the muster room are two American flags, framed photographs of the police commissioner and his chiefs, wanted posters, and announcements of births, deaths, and fund-raisers in the police community. A large wooden desk, almost like a judge's bench but longer, is home for the lieutenants, sergeants, and cops who work inside the station house. A small desk sits to their right,

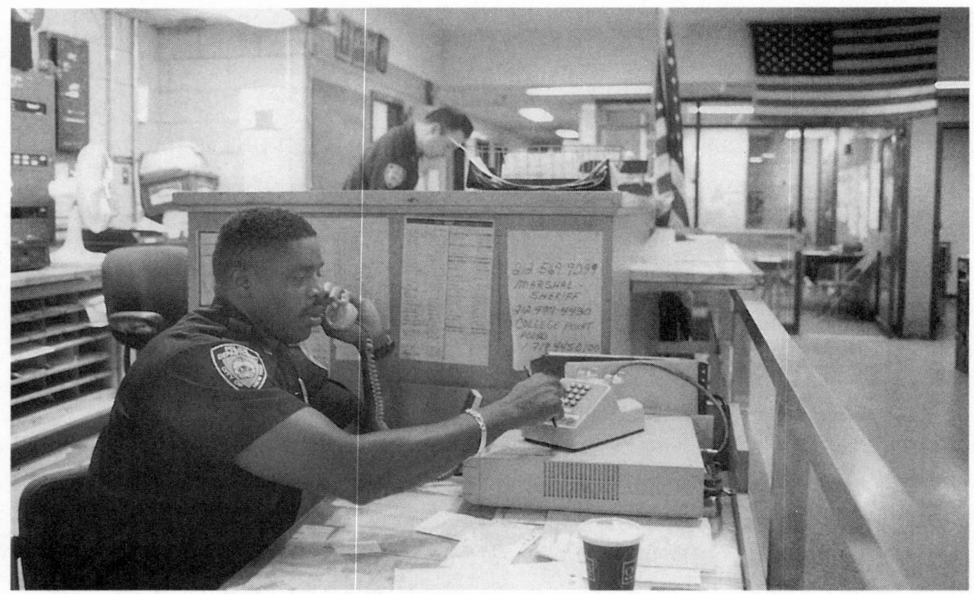

Officer Mayfield answers telephones at the 34th Precinct.

where Steven Mayfield and other cops take turns answering the old push-button telephones, handling community calls, which range from complaints about noise or double-parked cars to requests for advice or directions. Holding cells—where suspects are kept before they are bailed out or released or transferred to prison—are located in a small, windowless room next to the desks.

"People think that police have the answer to everything," Mayfield says.

A sergeant agrees. "Sometimes when someone doesn't come home, a family member calls the precinct and says, 'My brother hasn't come home yet. Was he locked up?'"

The precinct has a few unwanted residents. When Police Officer Dave Lawrence serves carrot cake for his birthday on paper plates, a mouse zips past his feet and under a desk. "That mouse'll be eating good tonight!" Lawrence exclaims as a crumb rolls under the desk.

The world of a cop is unpredictable because people are unpredictable. "There is no typical day," comments Sergeant Paul Crowley.

A million 911 calls are made each year in New York City. Central dispatchers take the calls and send the information via radio to the appropriate city precincts, where it is relayed to cops in patrol cars or on foot. Four cars and numerous beat cops patrol the 34th Precinct twenty-four hours a day.

Officer J. R. Aponte

Sometimes emergency calls to the police can be silly. Mayfield was once called to rescue a cat from a tree. He did so, but the cat jumped right back into the tree. But other calls bring officers into deadly danger or sickening violence.

Officer J. R. Aponte once shot and killed a man. "It was a push-in robbery," he recalls. (In a push-in robbery, the thief knocks on the door and, when the victim opens it, pushes past him into the apartment.) Aponte continues, "The victim was outside the door and so were we. We saw the gunman in the apartment window. He probably heard us or saw us in the hallway. He shot at us. He had to know we were cops. Who else dresses in blue and carries a gun? We shouted, 'Police! Drop it, motherfucker!' What are you supposed to say?" he asks. "'Don't shoot at me anymore'? I was just shot at! I was so pissed off!" he exclaims. He and his partner shot and killed the man.

Sergeant Paul Crowley and his partner narrowly missed being shot while working the midnight shift. They ran after two young men who had just robbed drug dealers and were racing to catch a bus back to their homes in New Jersey. One turned and fired a sawed-off shotgun. The bullet passed so close to him, Crowley says, it sounded like the buzz of a bee. After a prolonged and exhausting chase, one of the perpetrators ran into the basement of a building. He was found hidden in a cabinet, wearing a cap that read STOP THE VIOLENCE.

One veteran cop, trying hard not to laugh, recalls the story of a woman who emptied a defective can of hair spray into the toilet bowl in her apartment. This lethal cocktail awaited the arrival of her husband, who sat on the toilet and lit up a cigarette. A spark fell in the bowl, and the volatile spray blew up part of the bathroom. Cops were called to investigate the explosion and aid the injured husband.

An even stranger story is of a man who was found in an apartment, shot dead in his underwear. When Sergeant Crowley responded, he discovered part of a finger stuck in the apartment door. One drug dealer had killed another but slammed the door on his own hand on the way out. The murderer went to the local hospital's emergency room, where he confessed to an interested police officer, who called the precinct to ask if anyone had found a finger. "Fingered by his own finger!" exclaims Sergeant Crowley.

The precinct's saddest and most unfortunate story took place in October 1993. Mayfield and several of his colleagues joined a "tag and tow" operation to rid the streets of double-parked cars. Seven or eight tow trucks arrived in the neighborhood, escorted by the police officers, who gave out summonses and protected the truck drivers from the wrath of residents. Just before 10 P.M. that Tuesday night, as the trucks began to haul away illegally parked cars, the police came across an unoccupied car in the middle of the street, its radio blasting.

"There were about fifteen Hispanic males standing against the wall nearby," Mayfield recalls. "We asked who owned the car. Nobody stepped forward. The car was summonsed and it was prepared to be towed, when a guy confronted me."

As Mayfield talked to the man, another man jumped in the car and sped off.

"When that happened, the guys standing by the wall began cheering," Mayfield recalls. "They were happy that their friend got away. It was no big thing to me. You win some, you lose some. We gave these guys a lawful order to disperse. They were blocking the sidewalk and they were getting kind of rowdy."

Most of the men began walking away, but "one guy refused to move. And not only did he refuse to disperse, he took a stance at me with his hands up," Mayfield recounts, still sounding surprised. "I couldn't believe it! He went so far as taking a swing at me. I swung back and I connected. He went down. This guy had to be placed under arrest. You don't take a swing at a cop."

The man was arrested and handcuffed and placed in a patrol car. Four other men were also arrested by Mayfield and other cops. "The block had started getting really bad. People came from all over chanting things. And we realized that the situation had the potential to become a very bad one," Mayfield continues.

The cops were surrounded and outnumbered. Mayfield called for a 10-85 on his police radio, an urgent call for an officer in need of assistance. He alerted other police officers that crowd control was necessary. Housing Police officer John Williamson and his partner quickly responded to Mayfield's call for help.

As the cops stood together in a circle in front of 501 West 175th Street awaiting the arrival of a supervisor, Mayfield saw something flash out of the corner of his eye. "I'm telling the other cops what had just transpired, and all of a sudden I saw something come down from the building and heard this loud impact. Whatever it was, all you could see was a cloud of smoke," he says. A heavy object had been thrown from the roof of the apartment building at the cluster of cops.

Mayfield ran through the entrance and raced up to the roof. "Once I got up to the rooftop, I looked over and I could see cops on the ground below surrounding somebody and people screaming into the radio, 'Get us a bus [ambulance] over here forthwith, you got an officer down!' That really shook

Cheer rose as deadly blow felled young cop

By AL BAKER and PATRICE O'SHAUGHNESSY

A cheer went up when a heavy bucket hurled off a roof fatally struck a young housing cop Friday night in Washington Heights, witnesses and police said yesterday.

Police Officer John Williamson, 23, was hit on the head and fell to the street after a five-gallon plastic pail half-full of hardened spackling compound was apparently pitched off the rooftop of 301 W. 175th St. The attack came during a car-towing operation that turned into a confrontation between cops and residents.

As cops knelt to aid Williamson and Officer Christopher Bardio screamed, "My partner, you gotta help my partner!" about a dozen of the more than 100 people on the street "started cheering that he was down," said witness Carmen Jimenez.

Scores of detectives fanned out through the neighborhood yesterday searching for the suspect, as some residents mixed sympathy for the dead cop with complaints of harassment by the tow operation.

Trisi Marrero, 17, said she saw Williamson "lying on his back, blood coming out of his head. He was still. The blood was all around his head. No one deserves something like that."

Two vehicles were being hauled away when a hostile crowd gathered and confronted police and the tow-truck operators, said Lisa Daglian, a spokeswoman for the Department of Transportation.

Officers from both housing

cheered and applauded."

Housing police union president Timothy Nickels said: "When he fell to the ground, people started cheering, almost like someone hit a home run. To see a young cop lying on a gurney with his head smashed in . . . This is lawlessness."

Williamson, who was engaged to be married, lived with his parents, John and Catherine, and siblings Paul and Nancy in a home in Jackson Heights, Queens.

His fiance, Elizabeth Downey, 24, a nurse, arrived there yesterday, clutching a box of pink tissues. The couple had been dating for the last five years.

"He really looked forward

'DAMN GOOD COP:' Police Officer John Williamson.

A newspaper story about Williamson

me up and I raced back downstairs," he says, closing his eyes at the memory.

Officer Williamson had been struck by a thirty-pound bucket of Spackle, hurled from the roof by Pedro Gil, a twenty-two-year-old dishwasher who lived in the building.

"I can remember it so vivid like it happened yesterday," Mayfield says. "The impact from the bucket pretty much knocked Officer Williamson under the car. We had to pull him out. The bucket hit him on the top of the head and . . . the ambulance came and we got him to the hospital and his injuries were too, too—fatal," he says quietly. Officer Williamson died at the hospital. "And the thing that really disturbed me when it occurred, there were seventy-five to a hundred people in the street. When the bucket hit him, these people cheered. That was very disturbing. I said to myself, these aren't people; these are animals to react in a fashion like this," he says, shaking his head.

In his statement to the police, Pedro Gil said, "Some tow trucks came up and were ready to tow my friends' cars for nothing. Some cop came out and started getting nasty with me and my friend. He pushes us. A fight breaks out with the cop and a couple of my friends. I run up to the roof to get a better look at what's going on. Once up on the roof, I look over once. I see it's basically over. I see a white bucket on the roof. I picked it up. I threw it off the roof."

A plaque for Williamson at the precinct

Police Officer John Williamson was popular and friendly. He is remembered by fellow cops for teaching them how to dance to Spanish music, and for trips they took together to Great Adventure amusement park and to the casinos in Atlantic City. He always reminded other cops to wear their seat belts, and he would offer them rides home in bad weather. And he answered Steven Mayfield's call for help that evening.

"We later learned that as we were running up to the roof, the guy who threw the bucket off the roof ran past us into an apartment. And subsequently he fled the country to the Dominican Republic. When he got back to the United States, he was arrested. He was found guilty of manslaughter. I don't know how he was found guilty of manslaughter and not murder in the second. Murder in the second is acting with a depraved indifference, which means he was acting in a reckless manner. He didn't care." Mayfield adds, "And I don't understand why the jury didn't see that somebody throwing a thirty-pound bucket off a six-story building in the direction of nothing but cops had the intent to hurt someone seriously, if not kill them, which he did.

Two Dyckman Houses residents

"For a long time John Williamson's death bothered me. Because," Mayfield says, looking away, his voice breaking, "if you have any humanity, any emotions, if you have an ounce of feelings, you couldn't help but feel guilty. Had we not called for assistance, Williamson wouldn't have been in the situation and the position for that to happen.

"So, for a long time I had to deal with that and try not to feel guilty for what had happened, because it could have very well been me. It could have been anybody, for that matter. I felt the effects of his death for a long time, for about a year. It disturbed me. And to this day, it brings back feelings. It stirs up emotions in me and I feel very sad. We lured him to his death. Of course, we didn't. But I couldn't help but feel that way. I still deal with that, from time to time, when I think about it."

Mayfield was so disturbed by Williamson's death that he went to Police Department psychologists for counseling. A cop may request an appointment or be ordered to go by a supervisor. Mayfield sought counseling on his own.

"I know the potential of things coming off the roof is always there. Listen, this is New York City," Mayfield observes now. "Always be prepared for the unexpected. You never know what's going to happen. Just when you get lax and you think, 'What's the odds of this happening?,' that's when it's going to happen. Anything"—he sighs, then takes a deep breath—"is possible."

But Mayfield has seen a positive change in Washington Heights. "Unfortunately, we can't be everywhere," he says. "But we try to do the best we can.

Some blocks are still heavily infested with drugs. But as a result of our commitment to the community, these streets are coming back. And I think the neighborhood has come a long way. You can definitely see that the people are happy and thrilled about it. Now it's a different neighborhood in many ways. This is a working community."

A New York City police officer in 1693

THE HISTORY OF THE NEW YORK CITY POLICE DEPARTMENT

New York City police officers travel over six thousand miles every day along streets, avenues, highways, and even rivers. They drive patrol cars, boats, and helicopters, and ride bicycles, horses, and three-wheel scooters. They walk hundreds of miles of pavement, parkland, and walkways. They unwrap and eat hundreds of hamburgers, packages of carrot sticks, roast-beef heroes, and sticks of gum, followed by steaming cups of coffee, cans of soda, and bottles of water. Never mind the doughnuts. "I've had my share. I especially like Krispy Kreme doughnuts," Steven Mayfield admits. "I ate them before I became a police officer and I'll eat them after I retire."

In 1625, when the first law enforcement officer patrolled New York City, life was much different than it is today. Automobiles, radios, telephones, televisions, and even doughnuts had yet to be invented. No one could predict the invention of computers, the popularity of The Gap and *The Simpsons,* or that skyscrapers and taxicabs would one day dominate the city.

Then the city was called New Amsterdam. It was a Dutch colony and the residents were mostly settlers. Johann Lampo walked alone along Indian trails and muddy paths, settling minor disputes and warning residents of fires. Homes then were constructed of wood and heated by fireplaces, so there was always the danger of fire. Even the smallest blaze could spread and become

deadly. With no running water and no fire trucks, residents could extinguish fires only by throwing buckets of river water on the flames.

Volunteer lookouts replaced Lampo and they, in turn, were replaced in the 1650s by a paid group of eight men. These men carried green lanterns to illuminate the unpaved streets, and wooden noisemakers, called rattles, to alert residents to fires and Indian raids. They hung their lanterns on a hook by the front door of their watch houses to let residents know when they had returned from their rounds. Today, all New York City police precincts have green lights outside their entrances as a symbol of the vigilance of their watch.

The British took the colony from the Dutch in 1664, and their military began policing the area, now called New York. A forty-five-man volunteer nightwatch worked alongside the soldiers. These were local residents who could be called for duty at any time. This citizens' watch ended in 1734 and was replaced by a dozen hired men who now stood watch over a city grown to 10,000.

During the Revolutionary War, George Washington fought for Manhattan against the British army, which finally retreated in 1783. Policing was now in the hands of the Americans.

By 1800, sixteen constables struggled to keep order in the streets. Over the next several decades, an influx of immigrants led to overcrowded tenements, and crime—robberies, prostitution, and gambling—began to overwhelm the city. New York became the first American city to adopt a full-time paid police force. Wearing badges made of copper, a squad of eight hundred men called "coppers" began patrolling the streets in 1845. *Coppers* was later shortened simply to *cops*.

These men had many of the same responsibilities that Steven Mayfield has today: directing traffic, handling domestic disputes, and searching for lost children. In 1850, they were outfitted with uniforms. They were authorized to carry guns in 1857. By 1898, the Police Department was separated into precincts with one central commissioner, just as it is today.

In the late 1800s, the New York City Police Department was largely

Irish. The great potato famine in Ireland sent starving families in search of a better life in Boston and New York City. The women typically became housekeepers and maids and the men became policemen. Police work was coveted as a job that offered respect and security.

At the end of the 1800s and the beginning of the1900s, women, blacks, and Hispanics were slowly accepted into the Police Department. While most criminals were men, a fair portion were women, and in 1891 women were hired as police matrons to search and transport female prisoners. Police matrons wore skirts and handled station-house duties only; they were not permitted to patrol or to investigate crimes alongside their male counterparts. It wasn't until 1918 that the city's first six full-duty policewomen were appointed to replace men who had been drafted to fight in World War I.

New York City's first black police officer, Samuel J. Battle

When George García became a cop in 1896, he was the first Hispanic police officer hired by the city of New York. The city's first black police officer, Samuel J. Battle, received the silent treatment from his fellow officers after he was hired in 1911. Respected as a symbol of authority and achievement by the black community, Battle gained much esteem in his thirty years with the New York City Police Department. He would be the city's first black police sergeant, then first black police lieutenant. In 1920, Lawon Bruce became the first black woman cop.

The New York City Housing Police force was created in 1952 to focus on crime in public housing complexes. Housing Police are most often based out

New York City Police Department logo

of offices in a housing complex. They originally handled problems as minor as overflowing bathtubs. Now they handle arrests and domestic disputes, drug dealing, and every other responsibility associated with the Police Department. Steven Mayfield functions very much as a housing cop would, except he patrols other areas in northern Manhattan in addition to the Dyckman Houses.

The Transit Police force was formed a year later. The men and women who make up the Transit Police patrol subways throughout the five boroughs of the city, handing out summonses to people smoking on train platforms or arresting pickpockets, assailants, and fare beaters (people who ride without paying). They deal with any crime or emergency on New York City's subway and bus lines, including passengers who are ill. The Housing and Transit Police were merged in 1995 with the New York City Police Department.

The New York City Police Department has grown to seventy-six precincts. Cops work in neighborhoods where residents may speak Spanish, Greek, German, Russian, Arabic, French, Hebrew, Hindi, Swahili, Polish, Korean, Japanese, or other languages. The severity of crime and its impact are different from neighborhood to neighborhood. A rapist might target the affluent Upper East Side of Manhattan, while gangs and shootings dominate crime in parts of Brooklyn. One community may have an undercurrent of organized crime, while drugs, car thefts, robberies, and child abuse may plague other communities. The police have to specialize in combating the crimes that are unique to their areas.

Some cops dress in suits and trench coats and investigate organized crime, homicides, assaults, Internet child pornography, and more. They are detectives and are appointed by the Detective Bureau. A cop can qualify to become a detective after he or she has served with members of the bureau in special units that investigate guns, drugs, or robberies. Unlike crimes on television that are solved in an hour (including commercials), investigations can take weeks, months, or years.

A man or woman interested in becoming a New York City police officer must be a United States citizen who is at least twenty-one years old and who has sixty college credits or two years active military service. The applicant takes a written exam, physical and psychological tests, and if he or she passes, spends six months training at the Police Academy, attending classes in police science, law, and social sciences.

Mayfield hopes the Police Department will recruit more mature cops. "Maturity comes from within. You're dealing with people at their worst. It's stressful. And people don't call you up when everything is good and invite you over for Thanksgiving dinner," he says. "If you're not accustomed to holding down a job, and especially a tough job like policing, you're in trouble. You have to be mentally tough as well as physically. And I think the mental aspect is more important than the physical aspect of it."

Steven Mayfield is one of forty thousand men and women who make up the current force. He holds the rank of police officer. The next rank above is sergeant. A sergeant is supervised by a lieutenant, who reports to a captain. To be promoted to a higher rank, a cop must pass civil service tests. Above the rank of captain, positions are by appointment. Deputy inspectors and inspectors serve as the commanding officers of precincts. They are like school principals, enforcing the policies of the Police Department and implementing plans and strategies to combat crime in their neighborhoods. Above them are deputy chiefs, assistant chiefs, and chiefs, most of whom work out of police headquarters in downtown Manhattan. At the top of the police hierarchy is the police commissioner, who is appointed by the mayor. The police commissioner runs the Police Department and is responsible for setting and enforcing policy and procedures for cops in all five boroughs of New York City.

Precinct commanders are held personally responsible for crime reduction in their area at Compstat meetings with the chiefs and police commissioner. Compstat, short for *police computer statistics,* highlights crime patterns on maps at these high-level gatherings. Strategies are then discussed to address guns and drugs, youth crime, gangs, and other pattern types.

A pattern could be a string of robberies in elevators in Bronx housing projects or several rapes in Brooklyn or a series of car thefts in Washington Heights. The Police Department heads will examine the computer reports and pinpoint locations (buildings, stores, streets, apartments), day and time (does the crime occur on certain days of the week or at specific times?), weapons (does the criminal use a gun or knife and what type?), and details about the criminal (clothing, shoes, does he or she always say the same thing?) or the victims (are they men, women, children of a certain age or ethnic background?). A pattern begins to emerge. For example, victims describe a tall light-skinned Hispanic woman, always wearing dark glasses and carrying a green tote bag who enters elevators in housing projects, usually on Friday and Saturday evenings from 5 P.M. to 11 P.M. She rides only with elderly people. She carries a knife and demands money and jewelry. She always says, "Thank you. Have a nice day." Once a pattern is established, police can then focus on solving the crime. Instead of randomly driving around a neighborhood, cops can pinpoint their criminal and the location of his or her next crime.

Because of these innovative strategies, murders, assaults, car thefts, and burglaries have declined to levels not seen during the seventies and eighties. Experts say that the decrease is a result of smarter police work, plus more police officers on the streets, tougher prison sentences, stricter gun laws, and fewer people hooked on crack.

"It's very frustrating, very frustrating," Mayfield says, "when crime is at an all-time low because of the men and women out there creating this safe environment, and then you turn around and every mayor tells you that you don't deserve a raise."

Police officers are a neighborhood's first and most familiar link to law and order. Their occupational hazards include being shot, stabbed, bitten, or contracting hepatitis or AIDS by picking up needles used by drug addicts. They earn almost $32,000 to start, which increases to a base salary of just under $50,000 after five years. That equals $15 an hour to start, $24 at top pay, not including overtime.

"I can't think of any other city where the men who pick up the garbage make more than the people who protect lives and sacrifice their own, patrolling these mean streets," notes Mayfield. "Policing, in my opinion, is one of those occupations that's pretty hard to put a price tag on it. But my theory and my logic has always been to pay us something that's decent. And what we get is certainly not my idea of decent when cops in other cities are making seventy and eighty grand a year and they're doing half of what we do. But fifty thousand dollars a year!" he exclaims. "After taxes, it's not that much. The benefits and pension may be a factor in the long run, but we're living for now."

Some New York City cops, tired of the stress and the low pay, leave the Police Department to join suburban police departments on Long Island and in upstate New York where the pay can be $20,000 more a year under less stressful conditions.

But some of the job stress comes from actions within the Police Department. It has been pockmarked by corruption and brutality scandals over the last thirty years. In the early 1970s, the Knapp Commission, with police officer Frank Serpico as its star witness, detailed routine payoffs to police officers from store owners, drug dealers, and organized crime. The Knapp Commission alleged that more than half of the police force was corrupt and that corruption had been tolerated and accepted.

In 1992, the Mollen Commission was formed after six police officers were arrested for drug dealing. Cops testified about corruption and brutality. Two years later, cops in Brooklyn's 73rd Precinct were arrested for dealing drugs while on duty and officers in Harlem's 30th Precinct were arrested for stealing drugs and cash.

Part of the problem may be the lowering of standards for those hired by the Police Department. The many police jobs are hard to fill. Years ago, a traffic ticket could prohibit a person from joining the Police Department. Today, Steven Mayfield may find himself working with a police officer who had once been arrested as a civilian. Felony crimes, such as assault with a bat, reduced to the lesser crime of misdemeanor, may not prohibit someone from joining the Police Department.

Three separate and tragic incidents in the 1990s further tarnished the Police Department's reputation.

In December 1994, twenty-nine-year-old Anthony Baez was playing a game of touch football with his family in the Bronx. The football hit a police car, enraging Officer Francis Livoti. He arrested Baez's younger brother for disorderly conduct, and as Anthony tried to intervene, Livoti wrapped his arms around his neck and began to choke him. Anthony Baez died as a result of an illegal choke hold. Livoti was acquitted of criminally negligent homicide but fired by the New York City Police Department. He was convicted by a federal grand jury of violating Baez's civil rights and is now serving a seven-and-a-half-year jail term.

"Stupid," declares Mayfield. "That's one of those things that should have never happened. Baez died for something so stupid."

Another terrible encounter between the police and a civilian took place in 1997. Abner Louima was arrested in a street brawl in Brooklyn after police officers thought he had punched Officer Justin Volpe. Louima, a thirty-two-year-old Haitian immigrant, was tortured and sexually assaulted in the bathroom of Brooklyn's 70th Precinct. Officer Volpe later admitted to shoving the handle of a broom into Louima's rectum.

After that incident, Mayfield said that neighborhood residents called out to him and his colleagues: "Watch out! They might use a plunger!"

Mayfield reads an article about a cop arrested and convicted of attacking a Haitian man in Brooklyn in 1997.

"I'm humiliated that one human being could do something like that to another human being," says an angry Mayfield. "And what compounds my feeling is the fact that Volpe represented something that I represent. I'm appalled by the whole thing," he continues, shaking his head in disbelief. "It's disturbing. Words can't express how bitter I am as a result of what happened, because it's a reflection on me. People look at me in a different light, and people view me as an animal like he is for doing what he did.

"He lost it," Mayfield says simply. "How you could lose it to that degree is beyond my comprehension. Volpe's not the only animal that we have on the job. There's more animals," he admits. "And you know what the sad part about that is? It's going to happen again. People are not going to learn from it. It's going to happen again. It has not necessarily to do with the Police Department, but with the nature of people." Volpe pleaded guilty in the hope of reducing a life sentence and was sentenced to thirty years.

"But one of the things I try to get people to understand is don't judge all men and women based on the actions of a few. Judge us based on our individuality," Mayfield insists.

Another tragedy involved four cops from the street crime unit, which focus-

SPORTS ★ ★ ★ FINAL

KNICKS HIT THE COURT TONIGHT SEE SPORTS

'PAYBACK' TIME FOR GIBSON PAGE 47

MONICA TAPE TO BE AIRED PAGES 6 & 7

SNEAK PEEK AT YEAR'S HOT TOYS PAGES 30 & 31

DAILY NEWS

NEW YORK'S HOMETOWN NEWSPAPER

COPS FIRED 41 SHOTS

Bronx DA probes fatal shooting of unarmed man

SEE PAGES 4 & 5

A front-page story about Amadou Diallo

es on pockets of violent crime in the city. They spotted Amadou Diallo, a street vendor, leaving his home in the Bronx in February 1999. The cops were on the lookout for a serial rapist and they thought the African immigrant looked suspicious. In the shadows of a darkened doorway, Diallo reached for something in his pocket. The officers thought it was a gun. One shouted, "Gun!" and they all began firing—forty-one times in all. Nineteen bullets hit Diallo, who died from the wounds. It turned out the young man was carrying just a wallet and a beeper.

While most of the public was outraged, cops have different opinions on the shooting. Some say they might have reacted similarly in the quickly moving situation. Others are not sure; still others are too afraid to say. Some feel the cops lacked proper training and supervision. Others feel they simply made a mistake, calling it a tragedy, not a crime.

"I don't want to second guess anyone," says one veteran police officer.

"They were looking for an armed rapist," says another. "They had every right to be concerned for their safety. What *if* he had a gun? What then? We have another dead police officer?"

Afterward, people on the street said to Mayfield, "Cops are shooting at anyone! They'll shoot you forty-one times!"

"I don't like to play Monday-morning quarterback. I wasn't there," Mayfield says. "But forty-one shots at one person is remarkable. It took four guys firing forty-one shots to bring this guy down? Maybe those cops are in the wrong occupation. They should be selling ice cream or something. The cops say he made a couple of moves and they didn't understand his moves. People make moves sometimes that you don't know what they're doing. But why did it take forty-one rounds to stop this guy? If that's not excessive, I don't know what is."

The four cops were declared not guilty and cleared of all charges, including intentional murder.

Mayfield gets angry thinking about the decision. "The bottom line is it's a black man. I'm frustrated and angry about that because more times than I care to remember, blacks are the ones being shot," he explodes. "You think I'm not going to be enraged by that? Damn right I'm going to be enraged. Do I have a right? You're damn right I have a right to be. Police person or not.

"Racism," concludes Mayfield, "has to do with each and every individual. Some officers—you can't tell me they're not racist," he protests. "They feel threatened by the fact that there's ten guys standing on the corner. I understand that's not something to be threatened by. People have a tendency to hang out on the street corner, just congregating sometimes. It's their form of relaxing, exchanging news and gossip, and a general meeting place. Are some of them up to no good? Some of them probably are. But are all of them up to no good? No. Not everyone understands the reason guys hang out on the corner."

He sighs. "We are still recruiting from the human race. There are racist people and there are racist cops."

Cops have been accused of hiding behind the blue wall, remaining silent to investigators about any possible wrongdoing they may have witnessed. "The blue wall of silence pretty much exists," admits Mayfield. "There's a wall of silence in every occupation where people protect, support, and look out for each other. It depends on each individual. I'm not going to take the fall for

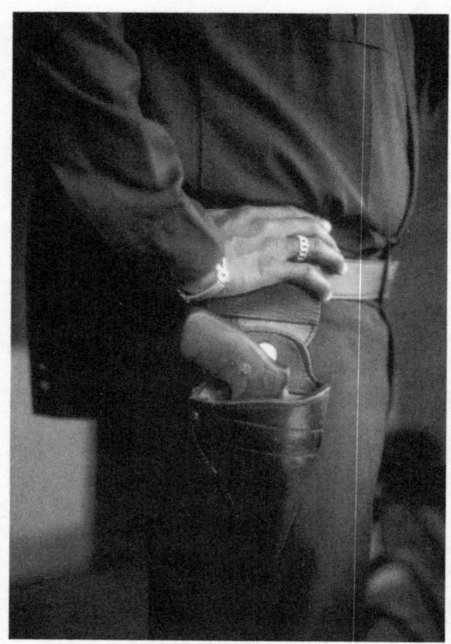

Officer Mayfield carries a .38-caliber revolver.

anyone. That takes away my dignity and self-worth. I couldn't care less how my colleagues would view me. I'm sure I would get ostracized," he surmises. "I'll support a cop if I think he or she is right. But if I think you're wrong, you don't have my support."

When an incident occurs involving the police, the public and media draw up sides quickly. Police officers are technically prohibited from talking to the news media about particular incidents because their comments could jeopardize the outcome of a criminal case. And to the public, their silence often implies guilt or disinterest when, in fact, they would be reprimanded by the Police Department for speaking. Newspaper, magazine, radio, and television reports often reflect comments by everyone but the police officers involved in an incident.

Many people on his beat are not happy to see Officer Mayfield. "You're the enemy out there, especially when you're out there walking around in uniform. You're the target. You never know what you're going into. There are a lot of situations where anything could happen. Officer John Williamson was killed by someone throwing a bucket of Spackle off a roof. A twist of fate and it could have been me," he says. "You have to be careful not to let your guard down too much because your occupation is a dangerous one and anything can happen."

Steven Mayfield rests his hand on his holster. "During the course of their careers, most officers don't have to use their guns. People with twenty-five years plus have never had to fire their gun," he says. "I tell people I hope that I never have to use my gun. Everyone wants to know how many times you've shot someone. I came close to shooting a kid once." He speaks quietly. "He was in an alleyway playing with a toy gun, holding it on another kid. But I never had to shoot anybody, and I thank God I didn't have to. And I hope never to."

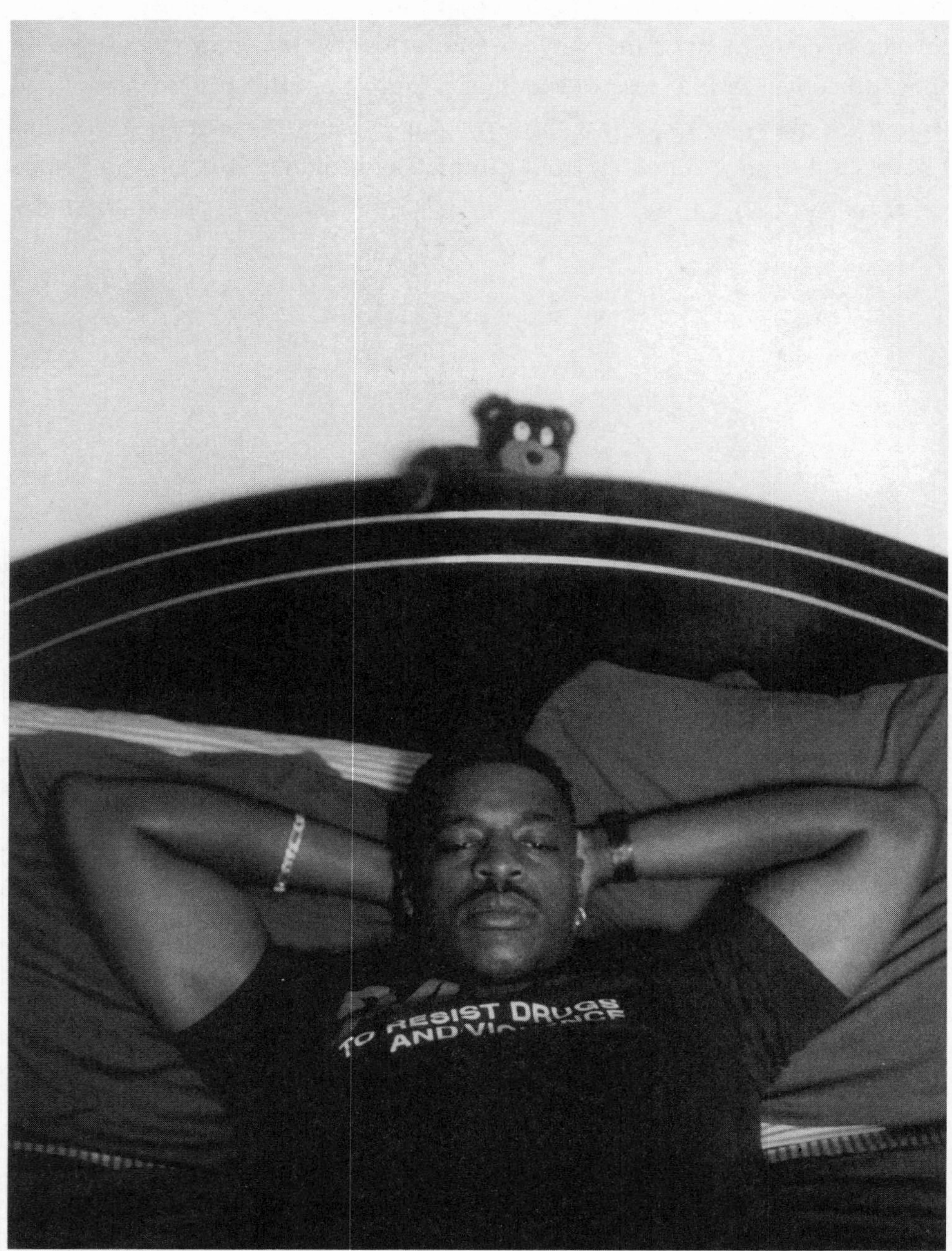

Officer Mayfield relaxes at home.

SUPERMAN AT HOME

After a week spent patrolling the Dyckman Houses, Steven Mayfield finally has a day off. He stretches out on the white love seat in his Harlem apartment, his feet dangling over the edge, his head resting on pillows. He sighs. "I've seen better days."

Like most other New York City police officers, Mayfield works the standard five days a week, eight and a half hours a day. He has Sundays and Mondays off. But during the summers, with New York City bustling with parades, street fairs, and festivals, he'll add another day of work to his schedule to earn overtime.

No matter how many hours he works, he rarely misses his daily visit to the gym, lifting dumbbells, bench-pressing three hundred pounds, and lifting free weights to improve his upper- and lower-body strength. "I like to keep in shape," the forty-year-old Mayfield explains. "You never know when you're going to need it on this job."

His days off are spent "relaxing, relaxing, and relaxing. Police work is very draining. It takes a lot out of you. And it's like any other job. It takes out as much as you put into it. It takes out a lot of me," he says.

Mayfield tries to schedule a haircut and a manicure every few weeks, and today he's lucky—his barber is in. Mayfield is religious about grooming: he carries a manicure set complete with scissors, clippers, and cuticle cream with him to work every day.

Back in his apartment, two weeks' worth of laundry awaits washing, windows need cleaning, paintings need dusting, rugs need to be swept with a

Mayfield lifts weights to stay in shape.

carpet sweeper, uniform shirts and pants are ready for ironing. If it's basketball season, Mayfield watches the Knicks on television, and during baseball season, he follows the Yankees. He listens to singers Billy Joel, Paul Simon, George Benson, and gospel singers the Winans, Mahalia Jackson, and Shirley Caesar. He does a wonderful impression of Paul Simon singing one of his hits, "Kodachrome," shaking his hips to the chorus, and adds his own touch to Elton John's "Rocket Man."

"Sometimes I need to be alone just to think things through," he says quietly. "Just to reflect." Mayfield doesn't share many of the details of his work with his family. "When you're living and doing it, you don't want to talk about it," he says simply and firmly. "I tell you, being a policeman's a good occupation to some degree, but one of the bad things about it is you always see people when they're at their worst."

He yawns and flips channels on the remote control from Ricki Lake to Montel Williams to Judge Judy and Judge Joe Brown. "When the public looks at police men and women, they fail to see the human nature in us. They see us as robots and insensitive and having no feelings whatsoever. There's been plenty of times I've come home and I've been sad as a result of something I may have seen," he admits. "Someone being abused emotionally or physically, it's bound to move you. An elderly person abused by a relative, a mother being abused by her son, somebody losing a loved one—I play it over and over in my head. And just being at various homicides and just thinking about having to go break the news to somebody—'Your daughter or your son just got killed.'

Mayfield gets his hair trimmed at a Harlem barbershop.

"That's just a hard thing to tell somebody. It takes a lot out of you," he says quietly. "You don't want to break down in front of anyone. Not that it's going to make you a bad person or a weak person," he adds, "but I'm supposed to be the law and I'm supposed to be stern and firm to some degree.

"Sometimes you can only make the decision that the job will allow you to make. You make use of the resources that you have."

His apartment is a New York City compartmentalized cement box with two bedrooms and a terrace. Mayfield's collection of African leather animals sits on and next to the television. African art and works by black painters decorate the walls. He is a big fan of Superman and wears the Superman *S* on a chain around his neck.

Mayfield slowly moves from the couch to locate his ringing cordless phone: it's his best friend, Harry Glenn, calling with a question about a police story he's read in today's paper.

Once Mayfield ends his call, he plumps the pillows and sweeps a few stray crumbs from the floor with his carpet sweeper. His dining-room table showcases his computer, fake flowers, and catalogs of homes. Mayfield is contemplating buying a home upstate. More than half of the New York City Police Department lives in the suburbs, with green lawns, little traffic, and quiet nights. "I'm tired of the city," he complains.

Mayfield keeps his apartment tidy by sweeping regularly.

A toy police car and a bear dressed in a police uniform are the only police-related memorabilia that Mayfield displays in his apartment. His numerous plaques for outstanding service are wrapped in plastic, hidden away in a cardboard box and cleaned a couple of times a year. Other than the car and bear, there are no signs that he is a police officer; his gun and bullets are nowhere in sight.

"I'm not a gun buff," he says. "I don't like them. And I don't want my nieces and nephews playing with toy guns."

Mayfield recalls the tragic killing of a kid who was playing cops and robbers with a toy rifle in a stairwell. A police officer was patrolling stairs in some housing projects in Brooklyn looking for drug dealers when a gun was pointed at him. He reacted. "The sad thing is that you can't go back and do it all over again. Was he wrong in what he did? You have some people say, 'Sure, he was wrong.' But was he really? No. In a situation like that, you can wait for that person to possibly shoot and kill you or you can take action first," Mayfield says. "I would not want to be that officer because wherever he is, he's got to live with the fact that he killed this kid. And even if that gun were real and that kid pointed it at him and he did what he had to do—it would bother anybody with a half a conscience.

"I can't think of anybody, other than a stone-cold killer, who would feel good and have no remorse for killing somebody. Cops don't look forward to killing people. We don't go to work every day and say, 'Well, let me see how many people I can kill,'" he says.

He rests his head on his arm, and noticing a few more crumbs on the floor surrounding his kitchen table, he picks up his carpet sweeper and sweeps them up. He checks his refrigerator—filled with cans of Pepsi and thawing chicken breasts—and decides not to cook. His mother's ham is too enticing, so he drives to her apartment a few blocks away.

He sinks into his mother's couch underneath the wall of family photographs. His gun, which he carries with him, is placed in a lockbox, out of the view of his mother and his nieces and nephews.

"I take all the bullets out so in the event that they do find it, it's empty. I keep them separate," he says, watching one of his nephews coloring in front of the television. "We ought to have gun-control laws. You got all these people with these gun clubs, and they all feel laws would infringe on their right to bear arms. These are all people who are in favor of something until tragedy strikes home. We have to do something," he insists, mentioning the shootings at Colorado's Columbine High School in 1999. "It's evident that we don't have enough control. Get these guns out of these young people's hands."

Mayfield notices a man with a gun on a television program, nodding his

Mayfield and his niece Alexis nap at his mother's apartment.

head toward it. "The kids are fascinated. Adults are the very people who teach these kids that guns are fun to have," he says. "Kids mimic their own parents and other adults.

"Toy guns look very real," he says. "They should be manufactured in a certain way. To color-code them, to prevent these tragedies from happening, to prevent kids getting shot by cops. Kids are walking the streets with their parents, pointing them at people. I've seen it. I got kids on my beat pointing toy guns at me and I say to them, 'Don't do that.' I'll look at the parents and say, 'You shouldn't allow them to do that.' Here I am, I'm a cop and you're allowing your kid to point a toy gun at me? But they don't care." He shrugs.

"Parents use cops in the wrong way. As they're walking down the street they'll tell a kid, 'If you don't straighten up, I'm going to get this cop on you.'

"And I tell parents, 'Don't tell them that because you're sending the wrong message. You're teaching them to fear me. Don't fear me. I'm the last person you have to fear because I'm here to help you.'"

His nieces and nephews fear him, though. "They call him the sergeant," his mother says, laughing. "Steven makes them listen. He calls them to the side. When they get a little wild, he gets on them. He has them scared to death of him."

Mayfield, who is single, keeps toys on hand at his apartment for his nieces and nephews: Elmo, Big Bird, and the Cookie Monster sit on his dresser. "The rubber duck in the bathtub is for me, though," he insists.

"Having no kids, I look at it as a blessing or a curse. I can't miss something that I've never had. I guess a lot of it is just that the right situation really hasn't come along," he admits. "And even if Mrs. Right did come along, I don't know at this point in time that I really want that to happen. I have no obligations in the sense of baby-sitting and providing for a child. It allows me to pick up and go. And I think that if it does happen for me, I would probably get in touch with a side of myself that I don't even know now," he adds. "It's amazing what a kid can do for a person's life. But it's not something that I really push. You get people out here having kids for the wrong reasons. And if I really wanted a kid, I can borrow one of my nieces or nephews for a couple of days, and then, when they get on my nerves, I can always return them."

Mayfield does his laundry at a local Laundromat.

He falls asleep on his mother's couch, and after he awakens, he returns to his apartment and to his laundry. He tosses the bag of laundry into the back of his car and heads to the Laundromat, where he sorts clothes by colors into washing machines. Since there is (thankfully) no Mrs. Right to question his odd assortment of old T-shirts, he takes them out of the dryer and folds them as neatly and carefully as if they were made of silk, including one, almost ten years old, that is filled with holes.

"But it has so many memories," he says defensively. "Well, at least it's clean," he adds.

Mayfield prepares to go out for the evening.

"I've been single for so long that being single is all that I know. There are certain things I'm looking for and certain things I'm not. And I pretty much like being single. Virgos," he explains, "are known to be temperamental and moody and to need their space. I know I can be stubborn and pigheaded.

"I just like the idea of being single and not being obligated to answer to somebody. It has its moments when things are not so great and so grand, when I find myself with a lot of free time on my hands, and nobody to spend my time with. I don't care how many people you have in your life, there's nothing like having that one person that you can express yourself to," he admits, "and just be yourself and just feel relaxed. But Mrs. Right can come and slap me upside the head with an open hand or with a frying pan and I probably still wouldn't know it. Mrs. Right has probably come in and out of my life twenty times over already, and I still haven't known it. And I probably won't know it.

"I have friends who married and they say, 'You know what? You're going to end up a lonely old man,'" he says with a laugh, but concedes, "And I tell you what. It's a scary thought."

Forgoing the T-shirts for one of his many custom-made suits, Mayfield gets ready for a night out with friends. He doesn't have a regular social routine, so on a night off he might go dancing or to a party or a concert.

His friend Harry Glenn says admiringly, "When it's time to step out, he'll go out and heads will turn. He's got quality jewelry, too. He goes to all the concerts, a lot of fashion shows. He knows all the great restaurants. But I don't see him married. I don't see him with any children. I see him being a free spirit," he adds. "It will be a *shock* to me if he gets married."

"In all reality, I'm a shy individual," Mayfield says, picking a piece of lint off his shirt. "But I like socializing. I like meeting people. I just think that New York has some of the most beautiful women; that's a bold statement to make considering I haven't been nowhere, but I just think New York has some of the most beautiful women."

He travels with buddies to Mexico and Toronto for vacations, and dreads the Christmas holidays. "I stay broke. With all my nieces and nephews—what I do is have them compile a Christmas list of items that they would like, and I ask them to select three items apiece," he says. "And so the only one that really I shop for, of course, is Mom. I make sure I get something nice for her."

His mother, packing suitcases for a trip back home to South Carolina, weighs in on the marriage question. "If he ever gets married, that would be a shock to me," Emma Mayfield says. "I ask the Lord to watch over him," she adds. "I say a special prayer that everything turns out all right."

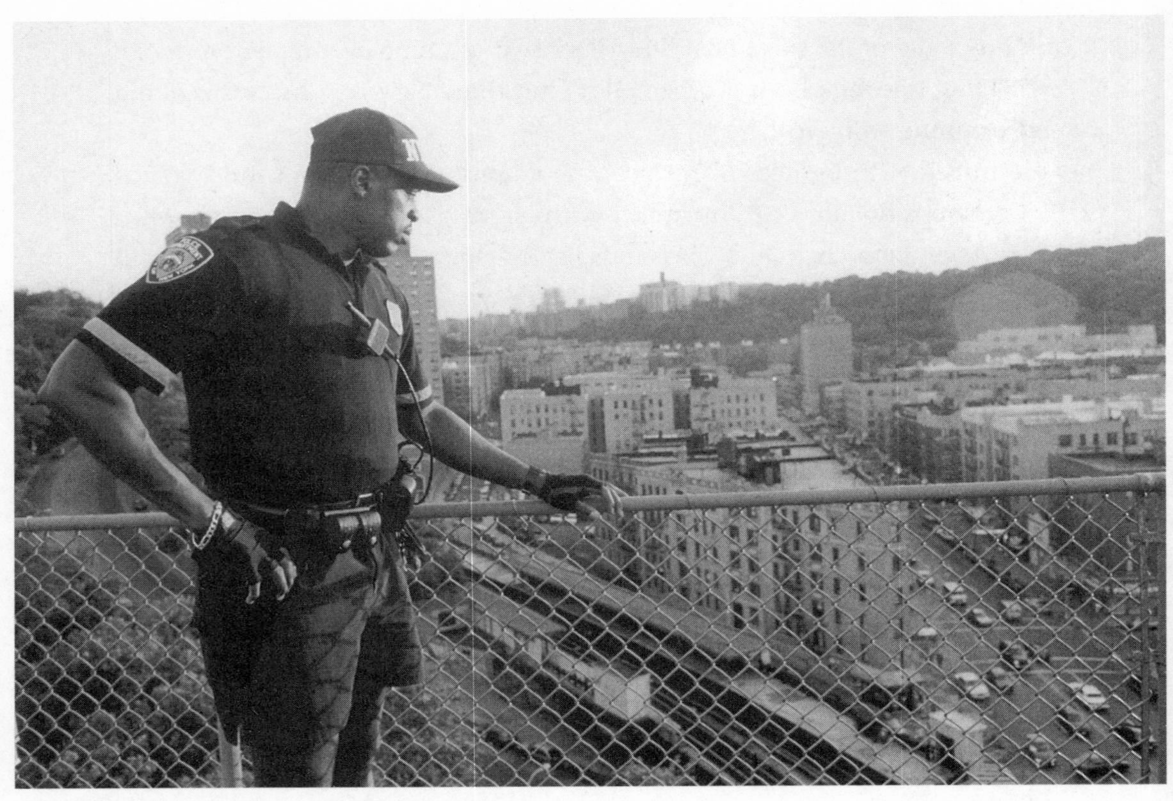

Officer Mayfield on a rooftop of the Dyckman Houses

6

COPS AND COMMUNITY

ANOTHER WEDNESDAY NIGHT

Officer Steven Mayfield, his hands on his hips, stares from a roof of the Dyckman Houses and points down to an apartment building two blocks away. On his thirty-seventh birthday, a young woman threatened to jump from that rooftop.

"She was twenty-four years old," he recalls, "wearing a nightgown and sitting on the edge with both feet hanging over. She was ready to jump over into the backyard. Her brother was lying on his stomach trying to convince her not to jump." Mayfield was called to the scene by the police dispatcher. He radioed back that she was a "confirmed jumper" and asked for help. The emergency services unit, a group of cops trained to deal with special emergencies such as this, set up an inflatable mattress six stories below. In the meantime, Mayfield had to keep the woman on the ledge.

"It could have been minutes but it seemed like hours," Mayfield continues. "I tried to convince her that she had a lot to live for. She had psychiatric problems. We didn't know what brought her to that point and we still don't. I had to talk to her to keep her distracted."

He lay on his stomach next to her brother and slowly crawled toward her. "'I'm going to jump!' she screamed. 'No, lady! Please! Not on my birthday!' I said. Other cops grabbed her before she dropped. I felt good that we were able to get to her before she jumped," Mayfield says. "But here I am risking my life to prevent this woman from taking hers. I try to be as careful as possi-

ble. You can't think about what could happen to you. You put it out of your mind until later."

Mayfield walks down the stairs and back out onto the street. With no crime in sight at the moment, he peers under his hat at people who pass by him on the corner of Dyckman and Nagle Avenue. Children eye him curiously, teenagers warily, women appreciatively, and young men suspiciously.

Officer Mayfield shows local students his handcuffs.

"Nowadays we're in an era when kids don't have self-respect, let alone give respect." Mayfield sighs. "They certainly don't have respect for cops. I had a kid one day—he was about thirteen—look at me and ask me, 'What you looking at?' And I said to myself, 'Wow! What an attitude!'"

After midnight in Washington Heights and Inwood, as in other city neighborhoods, there are kids circulating through the streets. Teenagers sit on park benches or cluster on corners in front of bodegas, some drinking, some smoking cigarettes, some carrying boom boxes. "I don't think there's a need for most of them to be out there. But as a police person, there's not a whole lot I can do about that. It shows the breakdown of the family structure, because parents should have some idea where their kids are, especially after midnight. They should keep better track of them," Mayfield says.

"If the kids are real, real young, then it is our responsibility to take them home and find out if the parents know they're out," he continues. "There's various reports we can do about child neglect when parents don't have control of a kid who's thirteen or fourteen who's out in the wee hours of the morning.

But all these parents don't have the necessary control they need to have over their kids, in terms of keeping some type of discipline and having them on a schedule, what time they should be in, and stuff of that nature. So the kids pretty much do what they want to do."

One student takes aim at Officer Mayfield.

WORKING WITH KIDS

Mayfield often speaks with neighborhood kids in schools, on work time and his own, about policing and the importance of education. At one school on Dyckman Street, inquisitive third graders clamor to see his gun, examine his bulletproof vest, and touch his nightstick and handcuffs.

"There's no need to be afraid of the police," Mayfield informs them. "We are here to help you. A gun is not a toy. I am not taking it out to show you. If you ever find a gun, please do not touch it. Make sure you find an adult," he advises as a student pretends to shoot him, her fingers pointed like a pistol.

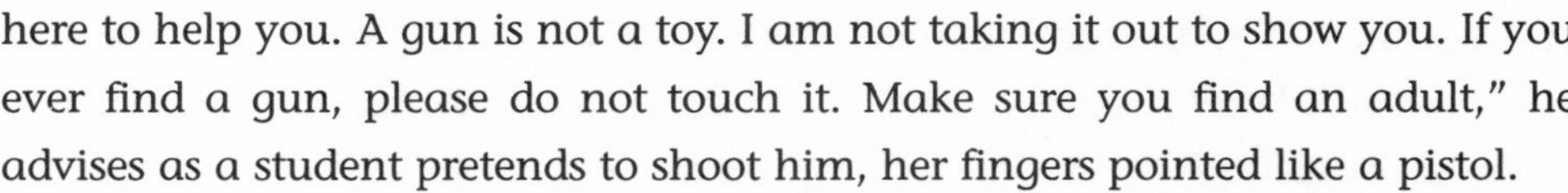

"How many times have you shot someone?" a young voice calls out. "What's that?" another asks, pointing to his handcuffs. "How old are you?" "Are you married?"

Many people—adults and kids—focus on Mayfield's gun. In his twelve years as a cop, Mayfield has never fired his gun except at practice sessions at the Police Department's firing range. Most New York cops carry the faster 9mm automatic weapon, which fires sixteen bullets and is easy to reload. Mayfield carries a .38-caliber revolver that holds six bullets.

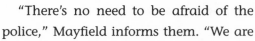

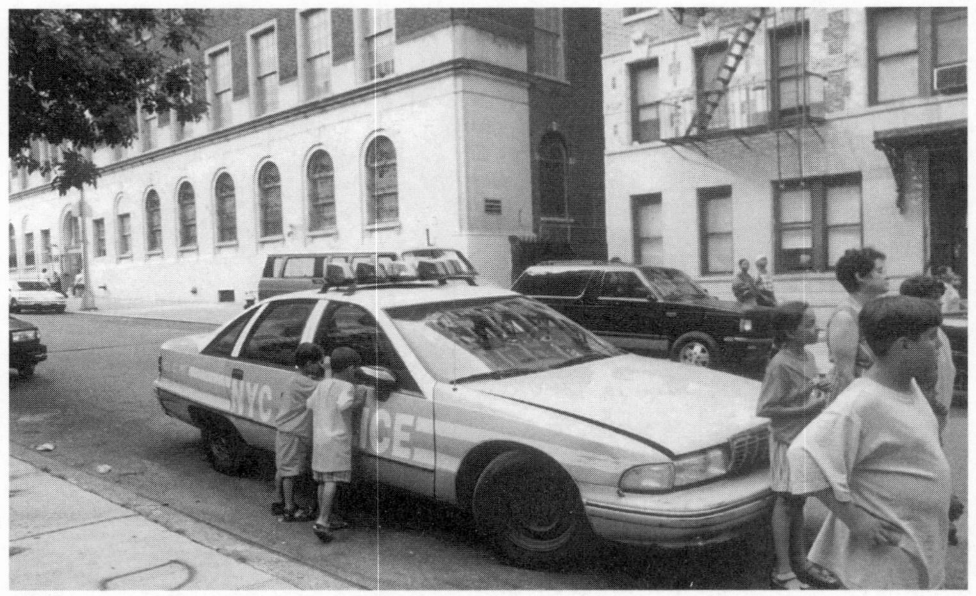

Neighborhood kids chat with cops.

"The reason I don't have the nine-millimeter," he adds, "is that I'm not a gun buff and I don't care one way or the other about guns. And I'd rather not go get trained all over again to learn to shoot a new gun. I'm content with my old reliable .38," Mayfield says, patting his holster. "I hope I don't ever have to use it."

"I've taken my gun out probably over a hundred times to protect myself. You don't know when a situation can become dangerous," he says. "It's police procedure to remove your gun from the holster when you answer certain jobs. Obviously, it's *not* going to be out if I'm standing over a person who's been hit by a car or issuing a summons for someone with an unleashed dog. But sometimes you're responding to a scene where shots have been fired or there's a call about a man with a gun—these are situations where you can get hurt. That's when I would have my gun out. You never know."

The New York City Police Department's *Patrol Guide* prohibits police officers from firing at a person who is running away or if the distance between them is judged to be too far or if there are people who might be endangered by gunfire. "Using your gun is a judgment call," Mayfield explains. "Each situation is different. If you feel danger to your life or anyone else's, you should have your gun out. It's your discretion. It's a judgment call."

Officer Mayfield holds up a practice shooting target.

During his time off, Mayfield also referees basketball games as part of a "Cops for Kids" program at a local church. With a black-and-white-striped shirt neatly tucked into black shorts and blowing a whistle, he trots up and down the court watching for fouls. And when a loss leaves an older teenager in tears, Mayfield is there to console him. "There's plenty more games of basketball out there," he says gently.

Wednesday evenings are reserved for the Law Enforcement Explorers program of the 34th Precinct, which attracts thirty teenagers from the neighborhood. Sponsored by the Boy Scouts and the New York City Police Department, it offers teenagers the chance to interact with cops and to learn law enforcement procedures and safety tips. The group particularly looks forward to field trips to the city jail at Rikers Island, the New York City Police Museum, and, Mayfield's favorite, Great Adventure amusement park.

Mayfield leads the Explorers with Tony Trinidad, the father of two daughters. "But you don't have to have kids to help kids," Mayfield says. "Some-

Steven Mayfield, basketball referee

times a person without kids has a different perspective because you're not in the mix of it every day."

The Explorer Scouts learn different techniques of police work, from stopping a suspicious car to catching a burglar in an apartment to breaking up a fight between a husband and wife. They take turns wearing a gun belt that's outfitted with a nightstick and handcuffs.

At yearly national competitions, Explorer Scouts are judged in how well they give commands, how well they work as a team, how they talk to perpetrators, how they go about finding and securing weapons.

Nineteen-year-old Explorers deputy inspector Ulysses Minaya says the program "teaches me responsibility, how to handle myself. It's an opportunity that many kids don't have. I'm working hand in hand with police officers." Minaya is now a student at John Jay College of Criminal Justice and plans on becoming an FBI agent. He has been accepted into the FBI's internship program. The son of a cardiologist and a nurse, he is one of eighteen children and a graduate of Mayfield's alma mater, John F. Kennedy High School in the Bronx. The training has helped him deal with others. "As a teenager, I see a lot of things. When my friends and neighbors are fighting and screaming at each other, I can handle the situation better. I separate people, put one in another room, speak calmly."

Community Affairs officer Tony Trinidad

The meetings begin with the Explorers standing for roll call and listening to announcements about upcoming events. The teenagers each pay a dollar a week in dues and face a uniform inspection by their peers and by Mayfield and Trinidad. Today, they're learning what a crime scene is and how it should be handled. Mayfield places bullets and ketchup packets representing blood on the ground. He tapes yellow crime-scene tape on two cars, including Trinidad's unwashed van. The Explorers break into seven groups: the one with the most correct observations will be the winner.

"Oh! This is just like *Unsolved Mysteries*!" exclaims one Explorer.

"This is a warning," intones Trinidad, a plastic straw tucked behind his ear and carrying a can of soda. He looks around for the straw. "Don't—touch—anything. Wait for the medical examiner."

"Preserve the area," warns Mayfield, turning in a circle so that everyone can hear him. "God forbid if the person does die, and you let everyone and anyone trash the scene. You have nothing to lose if you're in doubt and you let no one in."

He watches as they photograph bullets and ketchup packets. Two teenage boys waiting for their turn address each other as "nigger." Mayfield takes the two aside for a talk.

"'Nigger'—I don't like it," Mayfield says later. "It's disrespectful. It's become so common. They really don't understand it. I don't like it and I do the best that I can to discourage it. I try to make people understand that it is an ugly word. It's making reference to people of color. It means ignorance. It's lost its definition."

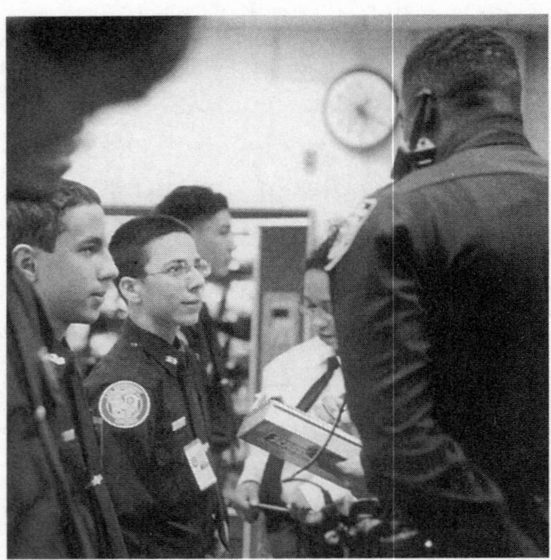

Officer Mayfield speaks with members of the 34th Precinct's Explorer Scouts program.

One girl walks around the suspicious car. "Be careful not to step on the ketchup packets!" Trinidad calls out, alarmed. "That's the blood."

Mayfield acts as the witness to the pretend crime and each group appoints someone to ask him questions.

"Do we badger the witness?" asks one enthusiastic teenager.

Later, the teens sit in the muster room underneath posters illustrated with black-and-white photographs of people wanted on outstanding warrants, fraud, and murder throughout New York City. Standing guard nearby are vending machines loaded with twelve different types of chips, plus M&Ms, Pop-Tarts, fruit pies, Chuckles, Swedish Fish, and Starburst for police diets. The scouts wait for the results of their competition.

Eighteen-year-old Ariel Morla, an Explorer for the last three years, talks about his friendship with Mayfield. He says of the older man, "He's nice to be around. He helps you with any problem you have. He doesn't make fun of

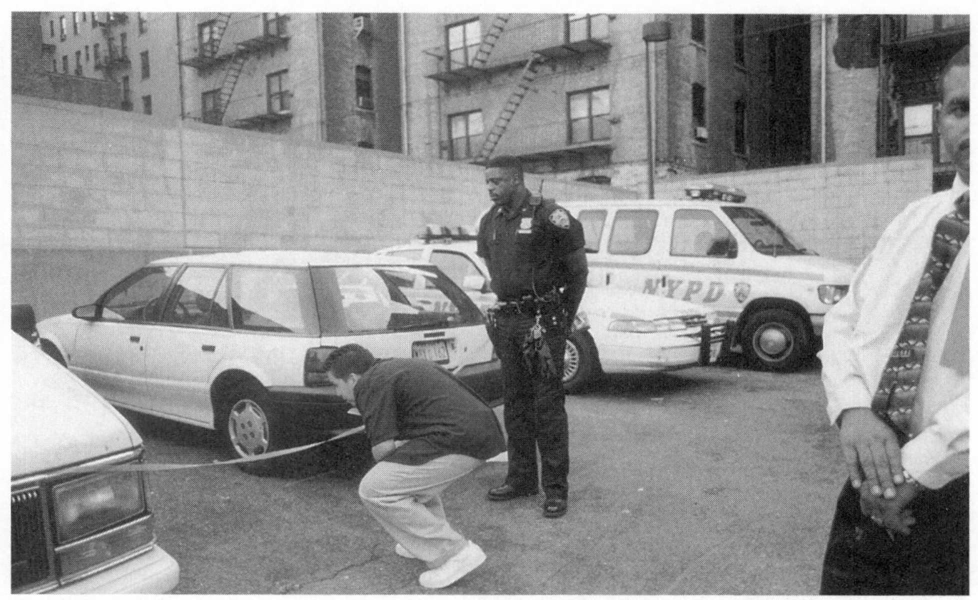

Officers Mayfield and Tony Trinidad supervise a group of Explorers.

you. He encouraged me to do good in college. He changed my life. He told me not to pay attention to what my friends say. 'It's your life.' He told me to be proud of myself and others."

Morla is majoring in criminal justice at Monroe College in the Bronx, planning to become a police officer. "I want to become a cop so I can protect my people and my city," he says. "The police officers make it better here year after year."

His mother works in a factory in New Jersey, making cosmetics from 5:30 in the morning to four in the afternoon. His father works eleven hours a day in a Bronx factory. Morla plans on moving to upstate New York to attend college, just as Mayfield did. "It'll be a new experience. He told me it will be different," he says.

Austin Lopez, fourteen, also admires Mayfield. "He's great. He's not uptight. He tells me to do the right thing. 'Don't follow other people. Do what you feel is right.'"

Doris Garrido praises him, too. "He's so nice. He does everything to get along with us. He's very helpful," she says. "I like coming here. Otherwise I would be sitting home watching TV. This is more entertaining."

Explorer Scout Ariel Morla consults with Officer Mayfield.

The sharp-eyed Minaya notes that Mayfield "is *neat,*" he says. "He likes to keep everything neat and sharp. I always ask him, 'When are you going to get married?!' He's too particular. It has to be his way or no way."

"I like working with these kids," Mayfield says simply. "A lot have expressed an interest in law enforcement. For others, it's something to do. Some are dealing with fears about police officers. We're here for them. When they have a problem at home or at school, they can trust us. We can provide some sense of direction or give an answer.

"'Education is the most important thing,' I tell them. 'It's the first step to any achievement.'

"You can only provide information and advice. You can't make a person do it. It's not like you can go to someone's house every day," he says. "Kids are going to do what they want to do. That's the bottom line. We don't have time to follow every kid. But you have to look at it this way: If there are fifty kids and you save one with some advice, you've saved one."

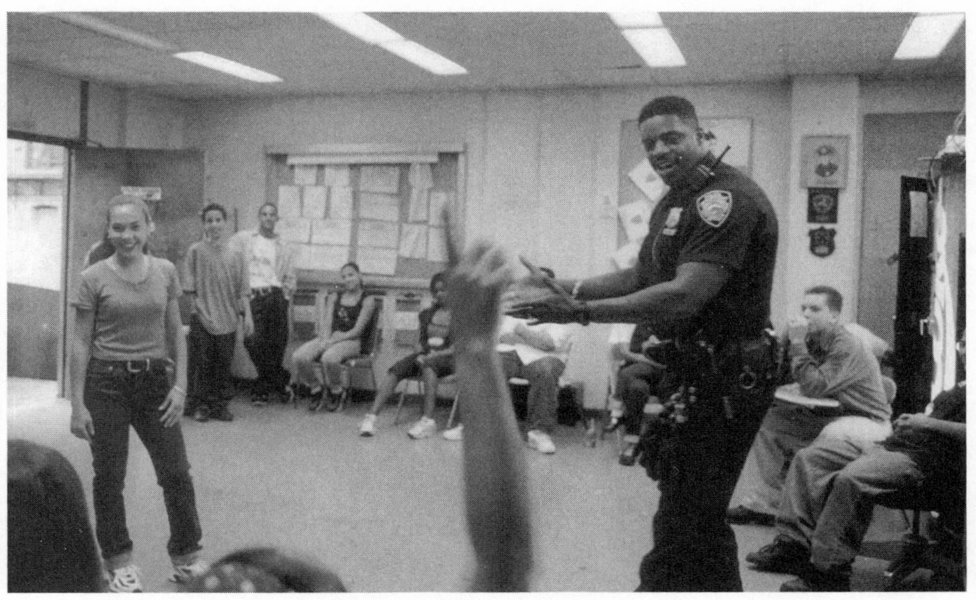

Officer Mayfield speaks at an Explorer Scouts meeting.

Mayfield is considering teaching or attending law school once he retires from the Police Department in eight years. "I'm not really sure," he says. "My goal is to be in law enforcement for twenty years and then work as an attorney, as a prosecutor, and after that, a teacher. Maybe I'll go back to school and get my master's," he continues. "One of the good things about the New York City Police Department is there are so many different avenues and so many different units you can try to get into."

He's considered a promotion to sergeant, but "I'm happy where I am. I'm not contemplating narcotics. I never ever wanted to do anything dealing with drugs. It's just dangerous. I'm content here, where I'm at, with the beat that I have."

Mayfield makes his rounds at the Dyckman Houses.

BACK ON THE BEAT

"You know," Mayfield says, looking over at two kids riding their bicycles toward the paths of the Dyckman Houses, "we live in a society where there's a lot of good people. And if you're not careful of the caliber of people and the type of people that you work around and with, the good people get lost within the bad. So you don't judge all the people based on the actions of some. And I certainly don't do that. I look back now at the death of Officer John Williamson and it was difficult because these are the very people that we serve and protect. And for one of them to go to that extreme and do what Pedro Gril did because he hates the police—I don't know how someone could do that. But once again, you can't penalize a whole community for the actions of one person."

Mayfield strolls past several senior citizens chatting on green wooden benches. "How're you all doing today?" he inquires.

"Fine. Fine. How you?" one replies, nodding, as Mayfield passes out of earshot.

"Mayfield," intones an elderly gentleman wearing a tan hat and wielding a worn wooden cane. "Everyone knows him around here. He's a very pleasant, professional young man."

His seatmate looks up from his newspaper. "Yep, he's good people. But," he asks hopelessly, "when is that man gonna get married?"

"All these po-lice," complains one woman, "they be beating up people every day, every day. What we need them for? They ain't nothing."

Another woman has had her wallet stolen. "Anybody seen Mayfield?" she calls out.

After twelve years at the Dyckman Houses, Steven Mayfield wonders what kind of impact he's had on the neighborhood. "Unfortunately, policing is one of those occupations, there's so many of us, and it's nothing but a system, and I'm nothing but a person with a number," he says, taking out his summons book again. "I'm here today and gone tomorrow, and for the most part too many people probably won't even remember me. They won't remember the impact that I had. And they might not remember the good things that I did. But they'll remember the bad things that I did if I do something bad."

He adds, "When I'm done with this job, I'd like to be remembered as someone who cared."

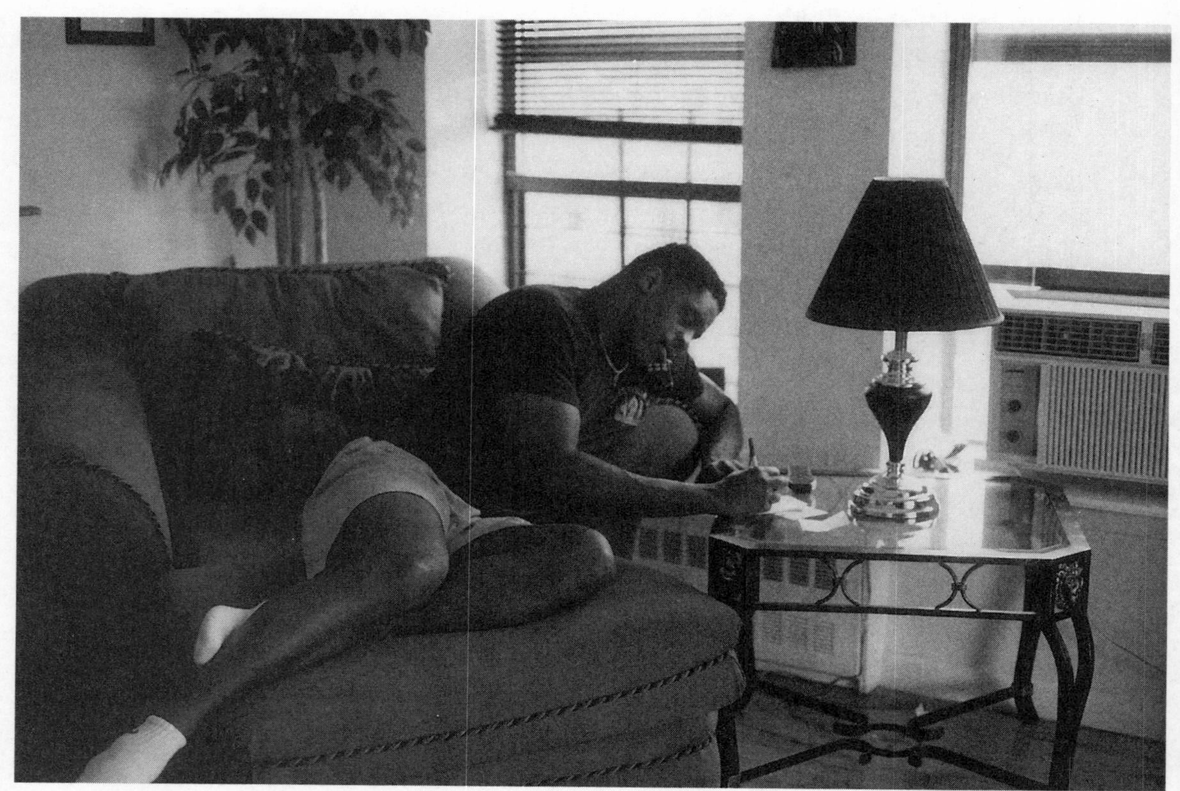

Steven Mayfield at home in his new apartment

7

MOURNING A HERO: A POSTSCRIPT

Steven Mayfield moved to another apartment in Harlem last year, and if he stands on the corner of his block and looks south toward midtown Manhattan, he has a clear view of the Empire State Building. His new home is in a six-floor walk-up and is kept as immaculately as his previous one. To celebrate his move, Mayfield purchased new furniture, including a soft brown couch patterned with lions, a chaise longue, African sculptures, and lucky bamboo plants. A colorful array of candles in different shapes, sizes, and smells dots the kitchen, and a large arrangement of dried flowers in matching shades of brown sits on top of the coffee table. The carpet sweeper is here, too, and the rubber duck has moved into his gleaming new tub.

On September 11, 2001, Mayfield finished lifting weights at a local gym when he noticed an unusual quiet. It was Primary Day in New York City, when the city's next Democratic mayoral candidate would be chosen, and something about the pattern of people in the streets alarmed him.

"I came out of the gym and you could see clear to the World Trade Center from there. People were huddled together in the street," he recalls, sitting at his kitchen table. "I overheard someone say, 'Did you hear what happened?' I heard another person say that a plane hit the World Trade Center. Then I heard another say it was two planes. Terrorism came to my mind automatically."

Mayfield ran home, jogging through the streets, to turn on his television.

Family, friends, and acquaintances telephoned him, wanting to be certain that he was safe.

"It really didn't dawn on me at first that my best friend, Harry, works down there," Mayfield recalls. Harry Glenn worked on the ninety-seventh floor of Tower One, above the floors that were hit by the first airplane. When Mayfield realized his friend was in danger, he called and called Glenn's office, reaching his voice mail and wondering if his friend was safe.

Two airplanes hijacked by terrorists earlier that morning in Boston had crashed into the towers. These city landmarks held thousands of offices, and that morning many people were at work there—in meetings, on the telephone, or eating breakfast. The impact of the planes, the exploding jet fuel, and the resulting fire weakened the structures, and as people in the streets watched in shock and horror, the towers collapsed. Nearly 3,000 people were killed, including sixty police officers from the New York City police department and the Port Authority of New York and New Jersey and more than three hundred firefighters.

Glenn's wife, Sharon, found her husband's name on a list of survivors that day and felt hopeful she would see her husband again. Mayfield didn't share her hope; he felt certain that Glenn would have called her if he could. They realized, a day or two later, that Glenn, like many others, did not make it out of the buildings.

"Anyone on a floor above the plane couldn't get out. They were trapped by the fire," Mayfield says, looking away from the framed photograph of the World Trade Center that hangs on his living-room wall. "I try not to take myself there. It's a painful situation. I can't imagine the chaos. I don't know if he jumped. No one knows where he was. He could have been on the fifth floor when it collapsed, for all we know."

Immediately after the collapse of the towers, and without waiting for a call to come in, Mayfield drove uptown to the 34th Precinct. "When I got to work,

Officer Mayfield makes note of his daily activities in his memo book. The George Washington Bridge is in the background.

it was chaos. We had never experienced a tragedy of this magnitude," he says. "A lot of people were sent downtown to secure the area and to aid in the rescue efforts."

Mayfield was assigned to the congested entrance of the George Washington Bridge, where he guided frightened motorists home to New Jersey.

In the following days, Mayfield and the rest of the police force worked twelve-hour shifts. Mayfield was sent downtown to direct traffic and handle crowd control at the site, reduced to concrete and dust.

"As soon as I saw the remains of the World Trade Center, I knew there would be few, if any, survivors. I had to see it in order to have closure. It was indescribable," he recalls. He was disturbed by tourists snapping photos. "Don't people understand that there are thousands of souls in there?" He adds ruefully, "Everyone wants a piece of history. People lost their lives out of hatred. Osama bin Laden is not good enough for death. It will bring comfort to me for maybe a second if he's killed. But it's not going to change the impact of things."

Six weeks later, Mayfield eulogized his friend at a memorial service at the same church where Glenn was married, not far from where the two best friends grew up. A framed photograph of a smiling Glenn and a poster of the Twin Towers were placed in the pulpit. Mayfield stood at the podium in his police uniform, speaking slowly and carefully, but with shaking voice and hands.

"No matter where our lives took us, I could always pick up the telephone and call Harry. He always had words of encouragement, guidance, and advice and he uplifted my spirits. I know many other people here feel the same way. Whenever there was bad news about a police officer, Harry was the first one to call to make sure I was safe. He always picked my brain about the latest police controversy," Mayfield said to the full church.

"I last saw Harry on August twenty-seventh, when we met for lunch. Our meeting was full of its usual laughter as we reminisced about old times, and we updated each other on family news. We had such a great time and he said we have to do this again next week. But that Monday was Labor Day and he had plans to be with his family. He reminded me that it was also my birthday.

"Harry called me every year on September third and this year he wished me a happy birthday and teased me about turning forty. So we promised to meet on September tenth, but we never had a chance to finalize our plans.

"He went to work on the morning of September eleventh to a job he loved at Marsh and McClennan.

"Harry Glenn, husband, father, son, brother, and my best friend, lost his life in a war of terrorism that is impossible to comprehend.

"Stories about the rescuers, the Fire Department and the Police Department, seem to have overshadowed people like Harry. Harry was a hero, too," May-

Officer Mayfield reads cards sent to the precinct after the September 11 attack on New York City.

field continued, taking a breath. The overflowing crowd in wooden pews murmured its approval with hearty amens.

"Harry's smile, his laugh, and his warmth are still with me. I wish he were here.

"The magic of Harry was he always had kind words for people. I'm not amazed at the stories of how he touched and comforted others. That was Harry. We should celebrate his life and feel lucky for the time we spent with him.

"Mr. and Mrs. Glenn, thank you so much for sharing Harry with the rest of us. I'm a lucky man to have such a great friend."

Mayfield presented Glenn's parents, wife, and son with a copy of his speech then left the church for a meeting downtown at police headquarters.

He admits to having trouble sleeping since Glenn's death. "I've had a couple of dreams about him," he says, back at his apartment. "No, I won't tell you how many times I've cried about him. It's a big loss. You don't replace someone like him. He was like my brother. You couldn't have a better friend. I miss his laugh and how he would pump me for information about the latest police thing in the news. I miss him saying 'Man, you crazy.'

"I don't think most people realized how much of a loss this is for me," he says, clasping his hands. "Friends come and go. There was a lot of love there. I wonder if he really knew how much I loved him. I feel a void."

While mourning the loss of his friend, Mayfield worked long hours of overtime alongside his police colleagues, safeguarding locations, responding

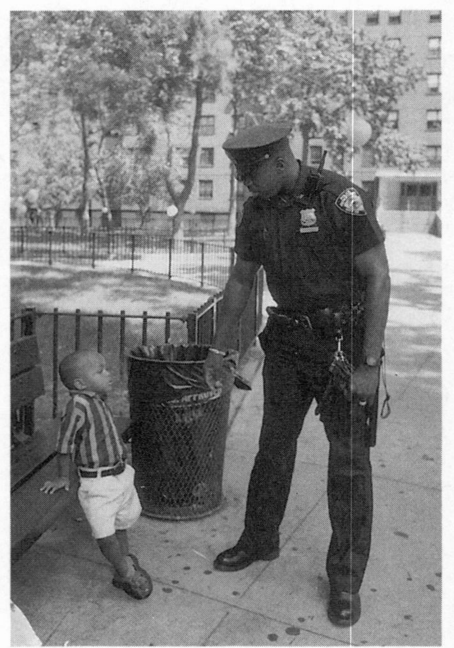

Officer Mayfield, who loves kids, chats with a young boy on his beat.

to alarms of suspicious people and packages, inspecting cars and trucks for bombs, and answering calls of suspected anthrax contamination by fearful upper Manhattan residents.

"We had no other option than to be more alert after what Osama bin Laden did," he says.

Mayfield says that Glenn's death has changed him. "I appreciate life more," he says. "Nothing's guaranteed. If it were me? I think I'm a decent person. I'd like to be remembered as a person who cared.

"People seem to embrace cops more," he says, finishing a meal of boneless spare ribs, shrimp fried rice, and Pepsi from his favorite Chinese restaurant. "They've been showing us more concern, respect, and empathy. People are just more sympathetic. It's a shame that it took a tragedy like this to show them our worth. People will continue to embrace us," he predicts. "But for some, it's already worn off. They've gone back to their usual disrespectful selves. I've heard people say, 'Oh, you should be doing something else. You should be down at the World Trade Center.'"

As New York City recovers from its devastating personal and economic losses, Mayfield is on his beat again. The rhythm of life in Washington Heights and Inwood and on his beat seems to be back to normal.

Mayfield looks down and notices something suspicious. He brushes a few pieces of lint from the front of his neatly pressed pants and then slaps a summons for double parking on another car windshield.

SOURCES

Jackson, Kenneth T., ed. *The Encyclopedia of New York City*. New Haven, CT: Yale University Press, 1995.

Lardner, James and Thomas Reppetto. *NYPD: A City and Its Police*. New York: Henry Holt, 2000.

The New York City Police Museum: www.nycpolicemuseum.org

GLOSSARY

Alzheimer's - a disease, mostly seen in older people, that results in mental deterioration and memory loss

beat - an area assigned to a cop to patrol

burglary - the act of breaking into and entering a home or place of business to commit a crime, such as stealing

civil service - work for the city, state, or federal government

civilian complaint - an official complaint made by a citizen against a member of the New York City Police Department

corrections officer - a person who supervises individuals who are awaiting or serving jail time

criminal mischief - intentionally damaging someone else's property

dispute - quarrel

domestic violence - physical or verbal abuse of family members or domestic partners

EKG - an electrocardiogram, the printout or reading from a machine that measures the heartbeat

felony - a serious crime, such as rape or murder, that usually carries a sentence in a state or federal prison

holding cell - a room designed for the temporary confinement of suspects

homicide - the killing of a person

manslaughter - the killing of a person without malice or deliberation

medical examiner - a physician who investigates the cause of death when a person has died unexpectedly or violently

misdemeanor - a crime less serious than a felony, such as shoplifting, which carries a sentence of less than a year in jail or a fine

morgue - the place where bodies of the dead are kept, and autopsied, before burial

murder - the deliberate killing of a person

nightstick - a club carried by a police officer, used to threaten or subdue suspects

911 - telephone number that summons police, fire, or medical personnel in an emergency

plea bargain - a negotiated agreement in which a defendant agrees to plead guilty to a specific charge in exchange for a reduced term of punishment

Port Authority of New York and New Jersey Police - a 1,300-person force that patrols airports, bus terminals, bridges, and rail stations in New York and New Jersey

precinct - the district that a police station house oversees; also refers to the station house itself

probation - a period of supervised freedom for a convicted offender

public housing - housing subsidized by government funds

robbery - the act of taking personal property from its owner by force or by fear

sector - a portion of a neighborhood that police patrol

sharecropper - a farmer who works the land of another in return for a share of the crop

Spackle - a powder that mixes with water to fill cracks and holes in plaster before painting

squad - a small, organized group

stop and frisk - action of a police officer when he or she has reasonable suspicion to stop a person to check for a dangerous weapon or contraband

summons - a written warning to appear in court; usually carries a fine

surveillance - close watch

suspect - someone who is suspected of a crime

INDEX

Page numbers in *italics* indicate photographs.

PAYSON
CUMMING ST
ACADEMY
VERMILYEA
DYCKMAN
AVE
STAFF ST
HENSHAW ST
MARTIN SQ.
W 206
W 205
W 203
ST
EXTERIOR ST
MAJOR DEEGAN

PAYSON
CUMMING ST
ACADEMY
VERMILYEA
DYCKMAN
AVE
STAFF ST
HENSHAW ST
MARTIN SQ
W 206
W 205
W 203
W 202
ST
EXTERIOR ST
MAJOR DEEGAN

U

V

W